T0318504

Cambridge Elements ≡

Elements in Current Archaeological Tools and Techniques
edited by
Hans Barnard
Cotsen Institute of Archaeology
Willeke Wendrich
Polytechnic University of Turin

KNOWLEDGE DISCOVERY FROM ARCHAEOLOGICAL MATERIALS

Pedro A. López-García
National School of Anthrology and History

Denisse L. Argote
National Institute of Anthropology and History

Manuel A. Torres-García
National Institute of Anthropology and History

Michael C. Thrun
Philipps University of Marburg

COTSEN INSTITUTE OF
ARCHAEOLOGY AT UCLA

CAMBRIDGE
UNIVERSITY PRESS

Shaftesbury Road, Cambridge CB2 8EA, United Kingdom

One Liberty Plaza, 20th Floor, New York, NY 10006, USA

477 Williamstown Road, Port Melbourne, VIC 3207, Australia

314–321, 3rd Floor, Plot 3, Splendor Forum, Jasola District Centre, New Delhi – 110025, India

103 Penang Road, #05–06/07, Visioncrest Commercial, Singapore 238467

Cambridge University Press is part of Cambridge University Press & Assessment, a department of the University of Cambridge.

We share the University's mission to contribute to society through the pursuit of education, learning and research at the highest international levels of excellence.

www.cambridge.org
Information on this title: www.cambridge.org/9781009506809

DOI: 10.1017/9781009181884

First published 2024

A catalogue record for this publication is available from the British Library.

ISBN 978-1-009-50680-9 Hardback
ISBN 978-1-009-18187-7 Paperback
ISSN 2632-7031 (online)
ISSN 2632-7023 (print)

Additional resources for this publication at www.cambridge.org/knowledge_materials

Knowledge Discovery from Archaeological Materials

Elements in Current Archaeological Tools and Techniques

DOI: 10.1017/9781009181884
First published online: June 2024

Pedro A. López-García
National School of Anthrology and History

Denisse L. Argote
National Institute of Anthropology and History

Manuel A. Torres-García
National Institute of Anthropology and History

Michael C. Thrun
Philipps University of Marburg

Author for correspondence: Denisse L. Argote, efenfi@gmail.com

Abstract: This Element highlights the employment within archaeology of classification methods developed in the field of chemometrics, artificial intelligence, and Bayesian statistics. These operate in both high- and low-dimensional environments and often have better results than traditional methods. The basic principles and main methods are introduced with recommendations for when to use them.

This Element also has a video abstract: www.Cambridge.org/EATT_DeniseArgote

Keywords: archaeometry, chemometrics, artificial intelligence, Bayesian statistics, spectral analysis

ISBNs: 9781009506809 (HB), 9781009181877 (PB), 9781009181884 (OC)
ISSNs: 2632-7031 (online), 2632-7023 (print)

Contents

1 Introduction

1.1 Overview of This Element

In recent decades, the number of archaeometric investigations that make use of physical-chemical techniques for analysis of the composition of various archaeological materials continues to grow, as evidenced by the increasing number of publications in this area. One example of this type of study is provenance analysis, which tries to relate archaeological materials to their original natural sources by discriminating their characteristic chemical fingerprint. In brief, it tries to determine the geological or natural origin of materials found in different archaeological contexts to establish the places of acquisition and production of the raw materials. The main objective is to determine ancient interactions between urban centers and long-distance trade networks.

We have chosen to approach this complex subject in two different ways, both based on very similar datasets. In this Element we take a theoretical and mathematical avenue, allowing the reader to amend and apply the discussed methods freely. In our companion Element *Machine Learning for Archaeological Applications in R,* we take an applied, more practical approach, allowing the reader to experiment with the provided datasets and scripts to be used in the R software package. These two Elements can be used independently as well as complementarily; throughout both, ample cross-references are provided to facilitate the latter.

A specific approach is to identify homogeneous groups of data in terms of their composition through the application of analytical instruments and quantitative statistical methods. In other words, it tries to find groups of artifacts that, according to their chemical characteristics, are similar to objects of the same source but different from the ones proceeding from other sources. Therefore, when clustering the data, the formed clusters should be highly cohesive and well separated (Baudry et al., 2010). Depending on the instrumental technique applied for the analysis of archaeological materials, the recovered data can be treated in three different ways: (1) as spectra; (2) as compositional data, given in proportions, percentages, or parts per million; and (3) as a combination of (1) and (2).

Case (1) considers high-dimensionality data ($n \ll p$) using full-spectrum readings, such as those obtained with Fourier transform infrared spectroscopy (FT-IR), Raman spectroscopy, or X-ray fluorescence (XRF) spectroscopy. For this type of data, the suggested approach is to apply chemometric techniques and unsupervised machine learning methods. First, the spectra are preprocessed by filtering the additive and multiplicative noise, correcting misaligned peaks, and detecting outliers by robust methods. Afterwards, the data are clustered using a parametric Bayesian model that simultaneously conducts the tasks of variable selection and clustering. The variable selection employs mixture priors with a spike-and-slab component, which make use of the Bernoulli distributions and the Bayes factor method to quantify the importance of each variable in the clustering.

Unlike the hierarchical grouping methods, where it is necessary to determine a proximity matrix using a distance function, the Bayesian approximation evaluates the posterior marginal in which the prior is defined as the product of a uniform discrete multinomial-Dirichlet distribution or the allocation prior (Partovi Nia, 2009). The posterior clustering is the marginal density of the data for the K known groups. Like agglomerative hierarchical clustering visualization methods, a dendrogram is constructed based on the posterior probabilities as similarity measures of the partition, with the advantage of having a probabilistic interpretation. Using a model-based dendrogram allows a criterion for cutting the tree in the point where the marginal posterior probability is maximized, determining the optimal number of clusters.

Case (2) contemplates low-dimensional data ($n > p$) where the recorded data have been converted to chemical compositions. For this case, the recommended approach is to adopt the methodology proposed by Aitchison (1986), which discusses some of the algebraic-geometric properties of the sample space of this type of data and implements log-ratio transformations. Respecting adequate preprocessing of compositional data, such as robust normalization and outlier detection, the use of model-based clustering that fits a mixture model of multivariate Gaussian components with an unknown number of components is proposed. This allows choosing the optimal number of groups as part of the selection problem for the statistical model. Mixture models have the advantage of not depending on the distance matrix used in traditional clustering analyses. Instead, the key point of the model-based clustering is that each data point is assigned to one cluster from several possible k groups according to its posterior probabilities, thus determining the membership of each of the observations to one of the groups.

For case (3), if reliable calibrations are available to obtain compositional data, this information can be combined with the spectra to obtain groups. For handling the data, a combination of chemometric techniques is used. In this case, a dependent variable y (or compositional values) is related to the independent variables x (or spectral values). The preprocessing is performed similarly as in case (2); this allows calibrating a model of predictive purposes that can discriminate those variables that provide significant information to the analysis, while eliminating redundancy of information as well as collinearity. Once the selection of variables has been made, a new methodology called databionic swarm (DBS; implemented by Thrun, 2018) is applied for clustering the data.

The DBS method implements a reduction in nonlinear dimensionality, exploiting the concepts of swarm intelligence, self-organization, and emergency (Thrun, 2018; Thrun and Ultsch, 2021a). A heatmap and a silhouette plot (Thrun and Ultsch, 2020a) are used as validation measures for assessing the quality of a clustering. In addition, a supervised index evaluates the efficiency of the classification, and finally the results are evaluated by a contingency table that shows the correct assignment of the observations to the groups. The procedure is applied to a set of archaeological artifacts, finding the exact origin of the samples according to their characteristics and thus proving its advantages over classic algorithms, such as principal component analysis (PCA).

In this Element, different alternatives for data management are presented for these different scenarios, emphasizing unsupervised techniques in which the group membership of the observations is unknown. When following any of these three strategies, it is essential to consider the principle of parsimony, to eliminate the improbable options in each of the situations and to focus attention on the specific objective, the types of variables involved, and the importance of not generating subsequent biases in the interpretations. Therefore, we place an essential emphasis on searching for clusters within the data, directing attention to diagnosis of data (i.e., detection of outliers), imputation of missing data, transformation of the original data, and validation of the results.

The Element sections present valid arguments for avoiding the conventional clustering and classification methods that are commonly used in analysis of archaeological materials; one such argument is that they have low predictive levels. The scripts for applying all the proposed methods to real data are provided in *Machine Learning for Archaeological Applications in R*, which also comprises an introduction to R, the computational environment in which all the codes are designed, as well as videos detailing the proper employment of these scripts.

1.2 Statistical Research in Archaeology: General Principles and Limitations

Statistics are a powerful tool for generating knowledge and have experienced an intense development from the origins of their use to the present. Currently, we apply statistics in all areas of knowledge and, in a decisive way, in the social sciences and humanities. With advances in computer technology and data collection, machine learning has become an integral part of all research, developing clustering models based on probabilistic principles and models that perform complex tasks. Among the problems addressed with machine learning systems and techniques are unsupervised, supervised, and semisupervised learning, each with its pros and cons. Although statistics are useful for manipulating large amounts of information, making comparisons and predicting results is also governed by a set of methods, rules, and theoretical assumptions that must be respected by the user. Moreover, to be successful in a clustering or classification, it is necessary that the studies of provenance consider several factors:

- sample size
- data transformation
- missing values imputation
- data diagnostics (outliers)
- dimensionality reduction
- variable selection
- classification algorithms
- model validation.

Sample size is very important in any research as it must be able to record the internal variability of the total population. That is why the sample must be statistically adequate for the estimates to be unbiased and consistent. A larger sample size will provide greater precision in the estimates of the various properties of the population under study, so it is advised that at least $n \geq 30$ (where n is the number of observations). For example, let us say that you want to sample an obsidian deposit in which there were several eruptive events; in this case, there would be greater heterogeneity in the data, so the sample size must be larger to obtain an optimal level of precision and thus be able to determine the variability of each of these subsources. Therefore, statistically speaking, the higher n $(n \rightarrow \infty)$ is, the more accurate the parameter estimates and the level of precision will be.

Data transformations are an important tool for correct statistical analysis of quantitative data. For instance, in distance-based methods (such as cluster analysis [CA]), if variables with wider ranges are not standardized, they will dominate the calculated distances. On the other hand, in chemical analyses, some variables are recorded in different units of measurement, so it is necessary to express the variables in standard units to make them comparable. Many debates in archaeology have occurred on the type of transformation that should be applied to date. In archaeometry, there are basically three transformations that are commonly used: Z score standardization/normalization (Baxter, 2003; Baxter and Buck, 2000), $\log_{10}$ transformation (Dean et al., 2007; Glascock, 1992), and log-ratio transformation (Aitchison, 1986; Egozcue Rubí et al., 2011; Pawlowsky-Glahn et al., 2015).

The Z score centers the variable at zero and standardizes the variance at 1, scaling the data to have the properties of a standard normal distribution with mean $\mu = 0$ and standard deviation $\sigma = 1$. Transforming data to $\log_{10}$ is assumed to improve the distribution of asymmetric or biased variables, preventing some variables from having a greater weight and having a dominant role in a classification. However, these two transformations assume that the data follow a normal distribution or approximate it; thus, when a significantly biased or multimodal distribution is presented, as in the case of chemical data, the results of these transformations may not be correct. Moreover, outliers can have an excessive impact on the Z score transformation since centering is done from μ and one or more outliers will have a strong impact on the estimates. In fact, most geochemical datasets do not have a behavior that approximates the normal or the logarithmic normal, even using different transformation methods; instead, they present problems of multimodality and the presence of outliers (Reimann et al., 2002). Therefore, our recommendation is to use Aitchison´s compositional theory (Aitchison, 1986), as will be fully explained in Section 3 of this Element.

In chemical analyses, it is common to encounter the problem of data recording values below the detection limits (VBDL) of the instrument, so researchers opt for data deletion or **imputation**. Deletion simply discards records that contain missing data, while imputation seeks to estimate the VBDL data using information from neighboring records or information present in other variables in the dataset. This procedure is considered aggressive; Baxter and Buck (2000) calls it draconian since, he considers, it leads to a significant loss of information. Instead, when the percentage of VBDL is low, it is recommended to use value imputation or substitution. This is based on the fact that compositional data provide information about relative values rather than absolute values of the components.

There are several robust alternatives to solve the problem of multivariable imputation. One of these is multiple imputation, where multiple estimates are combined to produce a single value, which will be used to replace the missing data and thus decrease the bias of the estimate. Imputation should be considered part of the investigation process for the purpose of reaching conclusions supported by solid empirical evidence. Therefore, caution should be exercised when a complete database is not available, as inadequate imputation methods, such as Mahalanobis distance, can lead to more problems than they can solve. Currently, procedures have been developed that have better statistical properties than the classic traditional options. For this, we recommend the "zCompositions" package (Palarea-Albaladejo and Martín-Fernandez, 2015), which implements several imputation algorithms, including Bayesian multiplicative replacement, the log-ratio expectation maximization (EM) algorithm, and the log-ratio data augmentation algorithm.

Another situation that often occurs is that there are observations that behave differently from the rest of the observations; that is, their attributes are considerably different from the rest of the values in the sample. These observations are known as atypical or **outliers** and can have a strong impact on estimates, as some methods base their estimates on the location and covariance vectors. However, although outliers greatly condition the results of some statistical metrics, this does not mean that they should always be removed. In some cases, outliers can also be valuable observations on their own because they can supply evidence about certain distributions in the data or about special circumstances in the sample set. In this way, it is necessary to have adequate methods for the detection of outliers. We must bear in mind that adequate diagnosis of the data is an important part of the investigation process since observations that have a strong influence on the modeling can skew the results obtained.

Because chemical analysis works with low- and high-dimensional spaces, it is important to consider **dimensionality reduction** (DR). There are two DR approaches that can improve predictive models by reducing data complexity, and they are known as feature extraction and feature selection. Feature extraction methods are used for displaying data in a low-dimensional space with the aim of creating a human-friendly visualization (Thrun et al., 2016); the most commonly used methods in archaeometry are those that apply linear transformations, such as PCA and linear discriminant analysis (LDA). Because these methods are linear, their effectiveness is reduced to datasets that are not linearly separable; however, many algorithms are unable to untangle nonseparable linear data. On the other hand, not all datasets are in linear space, as will be discussed more widely later in this Element. More efficient approaches to DR will also be described and discussed in this Element.

In archaeometry, it is common to observe that the multivariate classification of the instances is carried out in two main ways: either all the variables are included simultaneously or only a subset of them is selected arbitrarily. Neither of these two procedures is correct. In the first case, by having a greater number of components, a learning model tends to overfit, and its performance loses predictive power (Alelyani et al., 2014). In the second case, selecting a small number of components (e.g., bivariate graphs) without any statistical basis runs the risk of eliminating relevant variables, decreasing the accuracy of the learning model and the knowledge that can be provided by other variables. In statistical modeling, feature extraction consists of selecting the most important and/or the most relevant variables from a dataset; this eliminates irrelevant, redundant, or highly correlated variables, increasing the accuracy of the classification by using a criterion function that determines the "best" subset of characteristics. In this Element, robust **variable selection** methods, such as interval partial least squares (iPLS), are proposed.

Once the data have been preprocessed and diagnosed, the next important aspect is to consider very carefully the method(s) or algorithms to be used in the clustering and/or classification. In general, in the process of discovering if the data present a group structure, there are three different **classification methods** – unsupervised classification, supervised classification, and semisupervised classification – each of which has its pros and cons. In unsupervised classification or clustering, no a priori classes are established during the process. The partitions are established using a distance criterion to quantify the similarity between the observations so that observations within the same group are similar between them and different from observations found in the other groups. Supervised classification methods are based on a set of previously known classes for clustering the samples that are labeled as belonging to two or more classes, intending to predict the correct class of the data without labeling. A clear example of this type of classification is LDA.

Among the statistical multivariate techniques most used in archaeological research are PCA, CA, Mahalanobis distance, and discriminant analysis (DA). These methods are empirical and exploratory in the sense that the number of clusters and the class to which the objects belong are unknown beforehand (Everitt et al., 2011), except for DA, where the groups are known a priori and new observations are classified into one of them according to their attributes. Nevertheless, these classical multivariate methods present severe problems caused by the structures they find in the data. Moreover, most of these methods assume homogeneity of the covariance matrices of the groups, and that continuous variables must follow a multivariate normal distribution, assumptions that are difficult to fulfill. In addition, several publications that use these exploratory and classification methods have a clear absence of tools for data diagnosis, detection of outliers, and validation of the models, factors that are fundamental in data analysis. Let us remember and discuss these methods.

1.2.1 Cluster Analysis

Clustering is used to discover if the data show some type of recognizable structure that can differentiate and classify the individuals into significant ("natural") groups. The clusters are natural because they do not require a dissection; instead, they are clearly separated in the data (Duda et al., 2001). Using CA can result in a partition of the total set of sample units into homogeneous subsets with respect to their variables and with a notable heterogeneity between the different segments. In archaeology, several publications apply diverse clustering algorithms, with hierarchical clustering and partition-based clustering being two of the most popular approaches. However, knowledge of the theoretical foundations of clustering methods is limited, beginning with the lack of consensus about the definition of a "cluster" (Hennig, 2015).

An important part of this problem is based on the fact that a cluster depends on the context in which it works. Another main difficulty is that clustering is essentially ambiguous. That is, clusters can be interpreted in different ways, varying from application to application, and the results of the different clustering systems can be influenced by the quality and diversity of the clustering solutions (Ackerman, 2012). Therefore, although significant progress has been made in the investigation of clustering methods, researchers agree that the problem of clustering is still ill-defined (Adolfsson et al., 2019; Bouveyron et al., 2012). Other shortcomings of traditional clustering methods are that they are based on previously established clustering criteria and are seriously affected by the presence of outliers, which produces skewed groups. They also depend on the definition of "distance" used by each method, as well as the linkage option.

So, in circumstances where clustering is used to detect unknown groups, it is essential to assess whether the clustering algorithm is useful. For example, when using different clustering algorithms in the same datasets, one of the most obvious concerns is that the output clustering is not consistent, producing very different results for each situation (Alqurashi and Wang, 2019; Bolin et al., 2014; Wehrens, 2011). For this issue, we must consider aspects related to the formation of the optimal number of clusters and the allocation of membership of the samples to those groups, that is, we must evaluate the "quality" of the clustering. It is important to keep in mind that some clustering algorithms can detect groups even if the data do not have a clustering structure (Ben-Hur and Guyon, 2003). Therefore, choosing the proper clustering algorithm for the dataset turns out to be a crucial part of the investigation.

Classical cluster analyses have conflicts in finding the optimal number of groups and have a negative effect on high-dimensional data. Regarding this, Xie et al. (2008) were able to demonstrate that these methods underestimate the true number of clusters if there are a large number of variables with noise that can mask underlying grouping structures. Moreover, most of these methods force a fixed geometric model to form the groups without considering the underlying distribution of the data in the n-dimensional space (Handl et al., 2005; Thrun, 2018; Ultsch and Lötsch, 2017). For example, the cluster model of the Ward method is a hyperellipsoid. This causes a considerable tendency of the established clustering algorithms to produce mistaken results by creating incorrect cluster associations of samples or forcing the construction of nonexistent cluster structures in the data.

Other problems can also be identified in the most popular clustering algorithms, such as single-link and *K*-means. The first method is sometimes unable to reproduce a given cluster structure due to the well-known chaining effect, which tends to generate large diameter clusters with very dissimilar elements at the ends, and the second method provides weak cluster associations depending on the distribution of the data. Moreover, the *K*-means model has no notion of outliers and can provide poor cluster associations depending on the distribution of the data, assigning the points to a cluster even if they do not belong in any. It is also dependent on the initial values introduced, and the user must prespecify a number of clusters. This method assumes that the variance of the distribution of each variable has a spherical-like shape, which presents problems to group data where groups have different sizes, volumes, and densities.

Due to the lack of understanding of the statistical properties of the clustering methods, it is unfeasible to make formal interpretations based on the results obtained (Fraley and Raftery, 2002). To make a reliable inference in archaeometry, it is necessary to clearly understand the technical framework of the various clustering paradigms, as well as to recognize the fundamental differences in their behavior. Ackerman (2012) detected that the behavior of clustering algorithms is not stable when more data points are added to the analysis (naming such sets oligarchies); thus, it is essential to consider clustering methods that exhibit a high degree of robustness for oligarchies. It is also advisable to use an algorithm that does not assume a predefined geometric form so that the clusters obtained are statistically significant. Furthermore, it is important to ensure that the algorithm does not show erratic behavior when the conditions of the experiment change.

More exhaustive explanations of several inconveniences in conventional CA methods can be found in Fraley and Raftery (2002), Heller and Ghahramani (2005), López-García et al. (2019), Papageorgiou et al. (2001), and Ultsch and Lötsch (2017).

1.2.2 Dendrograms

In hierarchical clustering, the criterion employed to detect groups is the dendrogram or hierarchy tree. The dendrogram represents the ultrametric portion of the distance metric used and provides the means for establishing the number of clusters that could better represent the structure of the data, considering the way in which the clusters are nested depending on the selected distance measure and clustering algorithm. The tree is cut with straight lines to determine the number of clusters into which the set of objects is divided. Large changes in the fusion levels of the ultrametric part decide the best cut. However, an apparent separation into distinct clusters in a dendrogram does not guarantee that they are genuinely distinct (Papageorgiu et al., 2001). Furthermore, when cutting the dendrogram at different heights, clusters are merged or divided. In this way, the decision of the optimal number of clusters can become quite subjective.

The problem becomes more complicated when there are large datasets and the number of clusters is unknown. A larger number of objects to cluster requires larger distance matrices, which become more difficult to compute. There are several cases where the results of hierarchical clustering can be misleading, especially when there is no real class structure within the data. In addition, depending on the metric (measure of similarity or dissimilarity) and the linkage method used in the grouping, very different dendrograms can be generated. In addition, identifying outliers is a very difficult task because there can be outliers within each of the different groups found by the algorithm.

Examples of these problems are described in Thrun (2018), Ultsch and Lötsch (2017), and Ultsch and Thrun (2017). Ultsch (2005) created the Fundamental Clustering Problems Suite (FCPS), which consists of datasets with known a priori classifications. The FCPS was extended to high-dimensional cases and sampling in 2020 (Thrun and Ultsch, 2020b). All datasets specify clear cluster challenges, and several can be visualized in two and three dimensions. They are used to test the performance of different grouping algorithms; thus, if a clustering algorithm fails in the formation of natural clusters, this can be clearly contrasted with the a priori information available on each of these clusters.

As an example, the FCPS provides a dataset known as Chainlink in R^3 dimensions with $n = 1,000$ points and two classes (Thrun and Ultsch, 2020b). This dataset consists of two natural clusters (two rings) that are well separated in terms of distances and data density (Figure 1). If hierarchical clustering is applied to this dataset, using the Euclidean distance as a metric and the Ward algorithm as the nesting method, the dendrogram of Figure 2 is obtained. The clustering method determines the existence of two large groups, with one group containing a greater number of observations than the other. If the dendrogram is cut at 100, a greater number of groups with internal subdivisions in each of these are obtained, obviously distorting the original data space.

If the option to see the algorithm's assignment of the points to the groups is included, we can see that the algorithm determines the presence of two large groups: a small group with 299 observations and a large group with 500 observations and 201 misclassified observations (Table 1). If the nesting method is changed to the average method (Figure 3), the dendrogram configuration becomes more complicated, increasing the creation of groups.

Table 1 Partition of the observations of the Chainlink dataset.

clusterCut	a	b
1	299	0
2	201	500

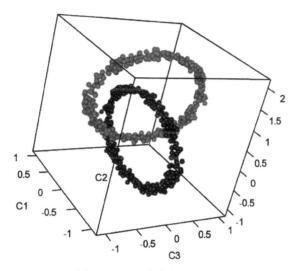

Figure 1 Chainlink dataset.

Source: Thrun and Ultsch (2020b).

Note: Colour version available at www.cambridge.org/knowledge_materials.

If the K-means algorithm, in which the groups are defined by the minimum distance of the observations with respect to the centroids using the Euclidean distance, is applied in setting up the number of groups (= 2), the graphic in Figure 4 is obtained. As seen, in addition to the overlap between the two rings, it is clear that the assignment of the observations to the clusters is erroneous because the proximity of observations in its vicinity causes an incorrect partitioning.

An example in archaeology is in Millhauser et al. (2011), who used PCA and Euclidean distance hierarchical clustering for the analysis of a group of obsidian artifacts from central Mexico. In the resulting dendrogram, the sources of Derrumbadas (Orizaba) and El Chayal (Guatemala) are nested together in a node, and Ixtepeque (Guatemala) along with Tequila and Magdalena (Jalisco) are nested at another node. The inability to differentiate between two geographically very distant sources turns out to be critical in a classification and, especially, in the

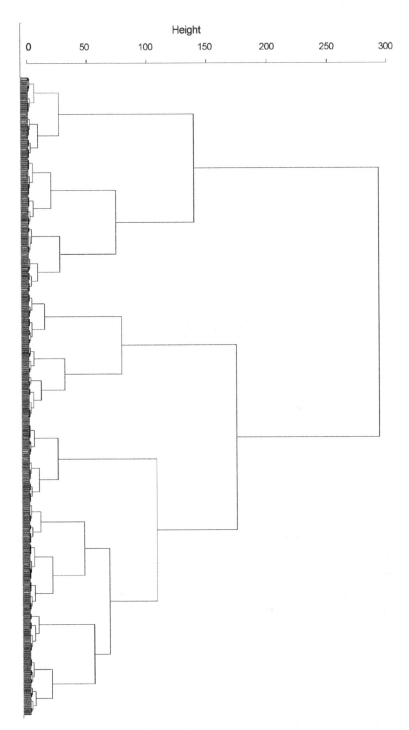

Figure 2 Dendogram of the Chainlink dataset using a hierarchical cluster algorithm (Ward algorithm).

Note: Colour version available at www.cambridge.org/knowledge_materials.

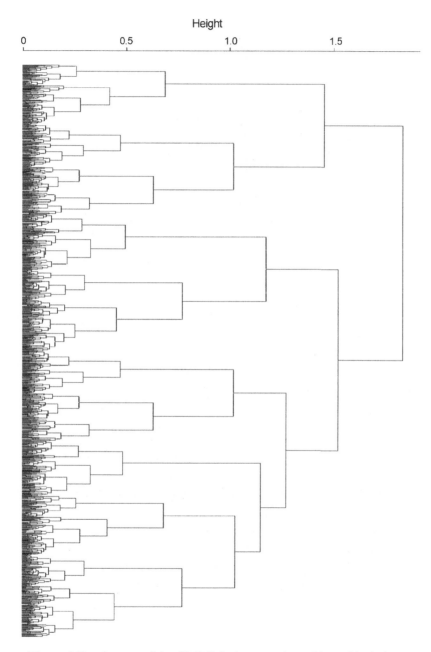

Figure 3 Dendogram of the Chainlink dataset using a hierarchical cluster algorithm (average method).

Note: Colour version available at www.cambridge.org/knowledge_materials.

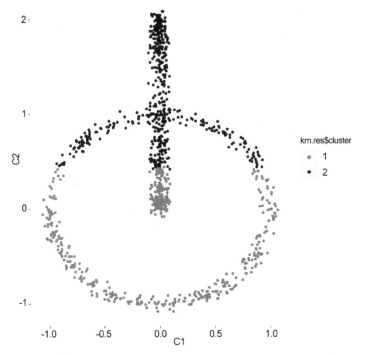

Figure 4 *K*-means clustering of the Chainlink dataset.
Note: Colour version available at www.cambridge.org/knowledge_materials.

inferences made at the archaeological level. All these simple examples account for the inherent problems associated with using grouping methods that depend on a distance metric and a nesting algorithm to form the groups. In many cases, the results of hierarchical clustering can be misleading, especially when there is no real class structure within the data. Besides, depending on the metric and the linkage method used in the clustering, very different dendrograms can be generated. Consequently, the underlying structure of the data can hardly be recovered. In addition, identifying outliers is a very difficult task. These and other issues make dendrograms a subjective means with which to analyze data.

1.2.3 Principal Component Analysis

One of the aims in archaeometry is to determine whether high-dimensional datasets reveal some type of structure in the reduced space to allow formation of groups of similar composition. For this purpose, linear DR techniques, in particular PCA, have been widely used in the analysis of archaeological data (Baxter, 2003, 2015; Doran and Hodson, 1975; Glascock et al., 1998; Santos et al., 2006; Tanasi et al., 2017). An advantage of PCA is that it is an exploratory technique that needs no distributional assumptions and can be appropriate for handling data that are inherently linear in nature. If the p-variables are highly correlated, the PCA transforms the original set of variables into another new set of uncorrelated variables called principal components (PCs). These new variables are constructed according to their order of importance in terms of the total variance collected from the sample. For a further explanation of this technique in archaeology, we refer the reader to Baxter (2003, 2015), Glascock et al. (1998), and Speakman et al. (2008); for a step-by-step example of the full calculation of a PCA, see Pielou (1984).

Before using this projection technique, the hypothesis of whether the data are linearly separable or not must be formulated. It is also necessary to analyze whether it is possible to adequately represent this information with a smaller number of variables constructed as linear combinations of the original ones. This assumes that the new variables must have a global correlation with the original ones. Ignoring this principle may result in errors such as overlapping groups, the formation of nonexistent groups, or the sudden rupture of points that originally belonged to a group. Any of these cases can completely alter the inferences about the archaeological problem (Ultsch and Thrun, 2017). In addition, the results of a PCA depend on the measurement scale of the original variables; in other words, if we transform the units of measure, the most likely outcome is that the obtained components will change.

Another important problem arises when the computation of the optimal number of components is not taken into account. In practice, the criterion used to choose how many of them are adequate to keep is based on the idea of preserving the fewest number of components that collect the greatest percentage of the total variability. Nevertheless, Chang (1983) stated that groupings in projections using PCA can occur in the last PCs, which are often not taken into account. However, in an experimental study that Ben-Hur and Guyon (2003) performed using a gene expression dataset, they proved that the total variance is a weak criterion for choosing the number of PCs when the aim is to cluster. An alternative would be their computation from a cross-validation (CV) analysis; for example, when the dataset has been segmented into a training sample and a test sample, the CV checks whether the results of the analysis are independent of the partition.

On the other hand, calculation of the eigenvalues and their associated eigenvectors is based on the estimation of the vector of means and the matrices of variance and covariance. Nevertheless, outliers can alter the covariance matrix given that they exert a force of attraction on the components, inflating the variance and distorting all the components obtained from this matrix. It is known that orthogonal contamination lifts the classical PC subspace toward the outliers and that bad leverage points tilt the subspace to accommodate all the outliers (Hubert et al., 2005). Moreover, the resulting model could explain the outlying objects more than the rest of the data (Daszykowski et al., 2007).

Konstorum et al. (2018) made a comparative study of linear and nonlinear DR techniques, evaluating their results by using several criteria. Among these were computation time, residual variance, two-dimensional visualization, and a newly developed comparison metric named neighborhood proportion error (NPE). The NPE measures the effectiveness with which each DR technique converts the proximity of the data points (within a subtype) from the input space to the low-dimensional projections. Konstorum et al. (2018) proved significant differences in the identification of groups obtained from the different techniques tested. This was evident in the calculation of NPE and the residual variance along with the two-dimensional (2D) graphs. The authors also showed that PCA was the technique that captured the greatest error, proving to be the most problematic technique regarding the separation of different populations, as it was difficult to clearly identify the boundaries between groups.

To exemplify certain problems of PCA, we used a dataset from the FCPS known as Tetra data (Thrun and Ultsch, 2020b), where $n = 400$, dimension $= R^3$, and classes $= 4$. The main problem with these data is that the groups almost touch each other in the three-dimensional (3D) space (Figure 5). By analyzing these data with PCA, we find that the proportion of variance explained by the first two components is 67.60%, and the overlap is very pronounced between Classes 1 and 4. Visually speaking, it is complicated to discriminate the groups if the ellipses of each group overlap with 95% confidence.

As a projection method, PCA is not capable of discriminating clusters with complex or entangled structures in a low-dimensional space. This has been demonstrated by Ultsch and Thrun (2017), who conclude that it is very difficult for this type of projection to preserve all the distances from high-dimensional space to the exit space, commonly represented in 2D or 3D graphics. For example, if PCA were to be applied to the Chainlink data (Thrun and Ultsch, 2020b), which are linearly nonseparable data, the proportion of variance explained by the first two components would be 67.42%. The projection of the points in the graph in Figure 6 is represented by including the class to which each point belongs. However, since the projection is in 2D, a significant overlap of points can be seen where the two links of the chain intersect.

Datasets can have nonlinear relationships. Therefore, if such structures in data exist and in order to overcome the limitations of linear transformations

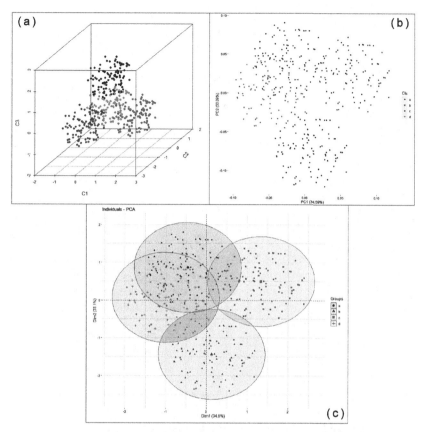

Figure 5 Principal component analysis of the Tetra data (Thrun and Ultsch, 2020b): (a) Tetra data in a 3D plot; (b) PCA of the Tetra data; (c) PCA with probability ellipses at a 95% confidence level.

Note: Colour version available at www.cambridge.org/knowledge_materials.

inherent in PCA, it is preferable to use nonlinear DR techniques. Some of these techniques are *t*-distributed stochastic neighbor embedding (*t*-SNE), nonlinear PCA, isometric feature mapping (Isomap), and polar swarm (*P*swarm). Finally, it should be noted that PCA does not explicitly define groups, and the main utility of this method is exploratory rather than inferential; its use without certain considerations leads to inferences without justification or to misinterpretation of the data.

1.2.4 Discriminant Analysis

As mentioned earlier, researchers commonly use exploratory techniques to determine whether data have a clustering structure. If the evidence confirms it, the data

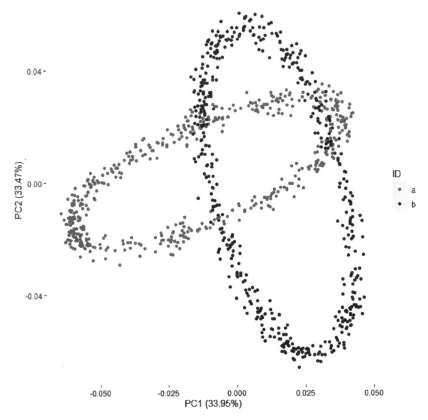

Figure 6 Principal component analysis of the Chainlink data.

Source: Thrun and Ultsch, 2020b.

Note: Colour version available at www.cambridge.org/knowledge_materials.

are assigned to the group with the closest proximity and, afterwards, are analyzed by means of an LDA with the intention of validating the data. This technique has been used frequently in archaeometry, with some examples published by Baxter (2015), Millhauser et al. (2015), and Munita et al. (2011). Also known as supervised classification, LDA is a probabilistic parametric classification technique. Its objective is the reduction of the dimensionality, seeking the separation or discrimination between groups through a discriminant function (generally linear) of the predictor variables using a class vector (Y).

Using LDA allows classification of new observations into one of the known groups. If the means μ_k, for $k = 1 \dots$ g, and the common covariance matrix Σ_k are unknown, which is usually the case, a training set consisting of samples drawn from each of the populations is required (Todorov and Filzmoser, 2009). Then, LDA can be performed in a linear or quadratic form, depending on the properties of the data. Either way, the theoretical assumptions of each technique must be considered. One of the assumptions of LDA is that the covariance matrices within each group should be approximately equal ($\Sigma_1 = \ldots = \Sigma_g = \Sigma$). If this assumption is not fulfilled, use of a quadratic discriminant analysis (QDA) is recommended. Nevertheless, an LDA can be affected by the scale/unit in which the predictor variables are measured. In LDA, if the sample size of the groups is small compared to the size of the p-variables, the inversion of the covariance matrices can become a problem and lead to singular matrices. On the other hand, if the number of variables is large, the QDA may have some problems when it comes to estimating the parameters of the separate covariance matrices within the groups (Baxter, 2015).

Another LDA assumption is that variables must have a normal distribution (Todorov and Filzmoser, 2009). Although Baxter (2015) states that LDA does not require this assumption when the purpose of the analysis is exploratory, if the LDA is used for validation purposes then this assumption is of utmost importance. Furthermore, a limitation of LDA as a pure classification technique is that the results are presented as relative probabilities. This means that if there are observations in the sample set whose class is unknown and who do not belong to any of the K-classes established a priori in the analysis, these observations will be erroneously assigned to any of the K-classes. Another drawback of LDA is that the prior probabilities are estimated from the relative frequencies of observations in each group; the estimates are based on the vector of means and the covariance matrices. If the data are contaminated with outliers, these will affect the estimates negatively (Hubert et al., 2005; Todorov and Filzmoser, 2009).

To exemplify part of the problems involved, we used the Chainlink data (Thrun and Ultsch, 2020b) to try to discriminate the two groups using LDA. In Figure 7, the degree of overlap between the two classes can be observed. If the confusion matrix is constructed to evaluate the percentage of correct answers in the classification (Table 2), the well-classified cases will be found on the main diagonal. Thus, of the 500 observations that belong to class 1, only 325 were correctly classified, resulting in 175 misclassified observations. Class 2 also seems to have a great degree of overlap, with 171 observations being correctly classified. According to the results, the classification accuracy is only 65%. As proven, the prediction error is quite high, showing that LDA is also not capable of untangling the two chain rings properly.

This shows that LDA is not adequate if the problem is nonlinear and if the assumptions of normality of the data and of equality of the variance and

Table 2 Confusion matrix constructed for
the classification of Chainlink data.

		Actual	
Predicted	**1**		**2**
1	325		171
2	175		329

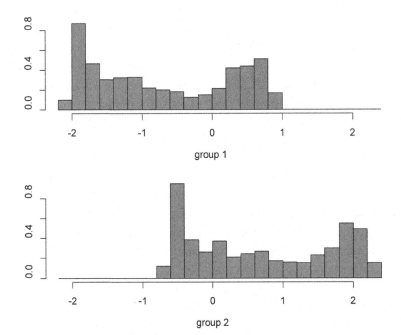

Figure 7 Histograms showing the overlap of the two chain rings.
Note: Colour version available at www.cambridge.org/knowledge_materials.

covariance matrices are not fulfilled. It can adversely affect the classification
process, as demonstrated by using data that are linearly not separable.

1.2.5 Bivariate Plots

In provenance studies, it is common to find bivariate plots using the original
concentrations of two elements or ratios of elements to visualize the formation of clusters. In the literature, there are several investigations that employ
them, such as Barca et al. (2019), Carter et al. (2017), Glascock (1994;
2011), Glascock et al. (1988), Joyce et al. (1995), and Moholy-Nagy et al.
(2013), to name just a few. However, it is important to keep in mind that if

bivariate graphs were used to discriminate groups between the different variables, it would be necessary to display a total of $n!/2!(n-2)!$ plots, making them impractical when the number of variables is high (Salem and Hussein, 2019). For example, if we have $p = 10$ variables, forty-five graphs would be plotted. In this kind of graph, it is usually difficult to perceive the trend of the points due to the existence of total or partial overlaps.

The same scenario can occur when multivariate analyses are used for the search of clusters. For example, Glascock et al. (1998) applied PCA to analyze materials from different obsidian sources measured with neutron activation analysis (NAA). Although the variance explained by the first four components is 96.43%, in the projection of PC1 vs. PC2, there is a slight overlap between the sources of Guatemala, Otumba, and Pico de Orizaba that can lead to confusion when determining the real provenance of the neighboring samples. The inability to differentiate between two geographically very distant sources turns out to be critical in a classification and, especially, in the inferences made at the archaeological level. To further assess the procedure of representing data in bivariate plots, we took on the task of using XRF data from different Mexican obsidian sources and displaying different combinations of components. The results were not positive (see Figure 8), as can be perceived from the large overlap between several source points.

In our general experience, bivariate graphs can give reliable results only if the number of sources or groups is small; if the number of samples increases, the overlaps will also be increased, especially if new information from other sources is added. To illustrate this last argument, we explored a dataset published in Tubb et al. (1980) that analyzed the chemical composition of Romano-British ceramics with atomic absorption spectrometry. This dataset consisted of $n = 48$ samples and $p = 9$ variables. The pottery came from five kilns located in three different regions. Their multivariate analyses suggested that the three regions were chemically distinct. In Figure 9, the totality of combinations of pairs of variables is displayed. From the thirty-six bivariate graphs of this figure, it is clear that only the combination of Al_2O_3 versus MgO gives a sign of the possible existence of three groups. The rest of the graphs do not present a clear clustering trend.

In the context of provenance or any classification method, if the data have a cluster structure, one expects to obtain compact clusters in the n-dimensional space and not clusters with overlapping, scattered, or sparsely separated clusters. These arguments highlight the inability of traditional methods to adequately recover the true structure of the cluster. On the other hand, what is the point of analyzing materials with expensive high-resolution techniques,

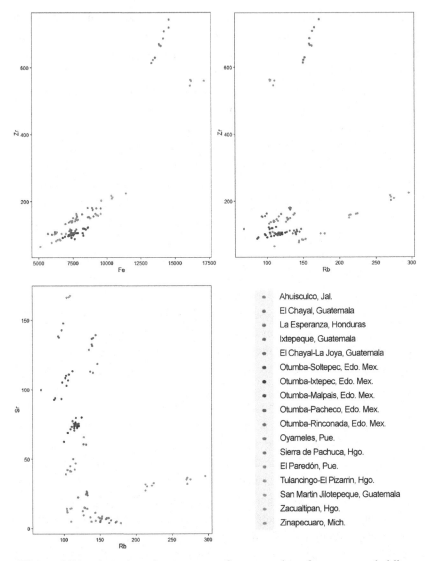

Figure 8 Bivariate plot of components from samples of seventeen obsidian sources and subsources measured with XRF.

Note: Colour version available at www.cambridge.org/knowledge_materials.

such as NAA or inductively coupled plasma–mass spectrometry (ICP–MS), if only two to four components maximum are going to be considered? Although in many cases the determination of groups has been based solely on bivariate graphs, we consider that this procedure is unreliable, and it is more advisable to operate with the full variability of the data or with proper variable selection methods to achieve consistent results.

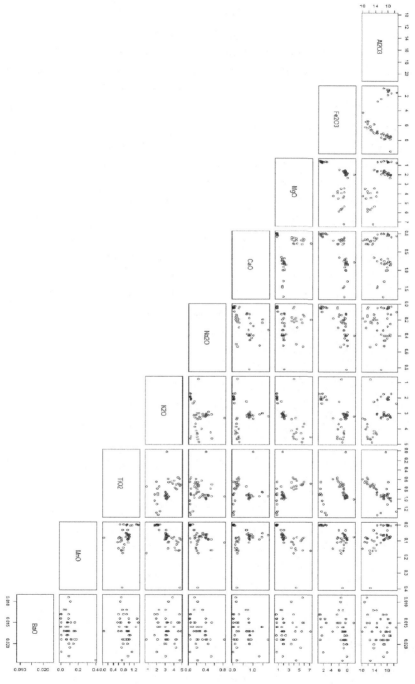

Figure 9 Bivariate plots for the total combination of pairs of components
of the Romano-British pottery samples.

Note: Colour version available at www.cambridge.org/knowledge_materials.

1.2.6 Mahalanobis Distance

Mahalanobis distance is another multivariate technique that is commonly used in archaeometry. The procedure consists of classifying a specimen as belonging to one of the K preexisting classes, estimating the vector of means and the covariance matrix (Σ) of each class for which the Mahalanobis distance is minimum (Glascock et al., 1998). The Mahalanobis distance statistic is used for three purposes: (1) to handle missing data by performing a type of data imputation (Sayre, 1976); (2) to detect outliers (Munita et al., 2011); and (3) to calculate the probability of individual units belonging to one of the G-groups found in the sample set (Glascock et al., 1998). For the imputation of values using the Mahalanobis distance, Sayre (1976) recommends substituting the missing data with a value that minimizes the Mahalanobis distance for the sample of the group centroid. However, there is currently a wide variety of imputation algorithms that show better performance than Mahalanobis distance, such as those displayed in Table 3.

If the intention is to use the Mahalanobis distance to calculate the probability of the specimens being members of one of the clusters, it is important to consider aspects related to this procedure. Shackley (1995) warns that, to obtain solid results with Mahalanobis distance analysis and not to incur an incorrect classification, certain conditions must be respected. One of the first conditions is that the n number of samples is large enough with respect to the number of p-variables; for example, $p > 3\,n$ (Bishop and Neff, 1989; Descantes et al., 2008; Glascock, 1992) or even $p > 5\,n$ (Harbottle, 1976). If this condition is not met, the phenomenon of "stretchability" may occur; Harbottle et al. (1976; cited in Glascock et al., 1998: 32) used this term to refer to the influence that an

Table 3 Imputation algorithms in R.

Algorithm	Reference	Package in R
KNN imputation	Hastie et al., 1999	impute
Multivariate imputation by chained equations	van Buuren and Groothuis-Oudshoorn, 2011	MICE
Hot-deck, k-NN, and EM-based	Templ et al., 2012	VIM
Bootstrap EM	Honaker et al., 2011	Amelia II
Random forest	Stekhoven and Buehlmann, 2012	missForest
Bayesian framework	Kropko et al., 2014	mi
Multiplicative approach	Martín-Fernández et al., 2000	compositions

individual specimen can exert over a group, stretching it in its direction in the n-dimensional space and forcing the inclusion of this specimen in one of the groups. This problem can be avoided if a CV method is used. However, this is a conservative approach to evaluating groups that may sometimes exclude true group members, as pointed out by Elson et al. (2006) and Lazzari et al. (2017).

If $p < n$, the variance–covariance matrix of the group would be singular, and therefore Mahalanobis distance would have no solution (Ferguson and Glascock, 2007). To solve this problem, Ferguson and Glascock (2007) proposed carrying out a DR procedure to calculate the Mahalanobis distance with the scores extracted from the covariance matrix ($\sum_k$) or correlation of the PCA components. This approach is based on the assumption that if the data show an underlying cluster structure, this should be seen in the first PCs (Elson et al., 2006). If the complexity of the data is high and the number of groups is large and with varied structures, Elson et al. (2006) recommend using the number of components that explain at least 90 percent of the total variation so that the Mahalanobis distance turns out to be a good approximation. Nevertheless, on many occasions it is necessary to include several components so that the sum approaches 90 percent of the explained variance.

Regarding the detection of outliers, Mahalanobis distance suffers from the effects of masking and swamping. Masking refers to the case when a data point is itself an outlier but the Mahalanobis distance labels it as not an outlier. This occurs when the peripheral observations bias the estimates of the mean vector and the covariance toward them; as a result, the Mahalanobis distances will be small. Conversely, in the swamping effect, the data point is not an outlier but the Mahalanobis distance labels it as an outlier. In this case, if a group of extreme values is present, the Mahalanobis distance can be increased by skewed estimates of the means vector and the covariance toward these values and away from other nonperipheral values; the resulting distance from these cases to the mean will be large, making them appear as outliers (Muñoz and Amón, 2013).

Most geochemical datasets contain outliers. Because the covariance and correlation matrices are very sensitive to extreme data, with the presence of these, variances tend to inflate and correlations tend to limit values (Todorov et al., 2011). In this way, it is very important that the data are contamination-free. On the other hand, it has been shown that the calculated components may not necessarily be the relevant components for the discrimination of groups (Chang, 1983). Therefore, the employment of Mahalanobis distance may not give the best results. A more developed way to reduce the impact of outliers is to apply robust multivariate methods of location and scatter (Hubert et al., 2005; Reimann et al., 2002; Rousseeuw and van Zomeren, 1990).

In addition to the mentioned difficulties, there is another more delicate problem when using Mahalanobis distance. This statistic presupposes the assumption of normality based on the relative probability of group membership (Glascock et al., 1998). To set up a threshold to determine which of the observations are potential outliers, as well as to assign the samples to the different groups, the Mahalanobis distance is based on the chi-square distribution. If the empirical distribution of the variables is normal, the use of this statistic is ideal; however, if the variables deviate from normality, the allocation of the samples to the reference groups will be performed inconsistently.

It should be noted that, in archaeometric data, the assumption of normality is rarely fulfilled, regardless of whether the original data have been transformed to a logarithmic basis or standardized. Violation of this assumption leads to erroneous assignment of the observations to a group, or to a percentage of the samples not being assigned to any of the recognized groups. In this way, before using the Mahalanobis distance, a diagnosis of the behavior of each of the variables must be carried out, such as via normality tests, to detect the presence or absence of symmetry in the values. In short, classical statistical parameters meet serious limitations when used for skewed data distributions.

1.2.7 Robust Clustering Algorithms

When dealing with quantitative archaeological data, one of the problems we encounter is how to look for meaningful structures in the data that can define the existence of groups of objects that are similar within a group and different from those found in other groups. In this regard, much has been said about the disadvantages of traditional methods of multivariate statistics. Therefore, when data are of low dimensionality, as in the case of chemical concentrations, we recommend using probability-based methods; these have increased the scope of statistical applications, as many datasets can be studied with great accuracy using probability distributions. Among these methods are finite mixture models, which are based on the conditional probability that all samples are generated from a combination of a finite number of Gaussian distributions with unknown parameters (Fop and Murphy, 2018). These methods have the advantage of adjusting a finite number of models to the same dataset and selecting from among the different models the one that has the best fit to the data.

On the other hand, when the data are of high dimensionality (with many more variables than cases), it is recommended to follow the variable selection approach. Partovi Nia and Davison (2012) implement a parametric Bayesian approach of spike and slab to reduce the effect of noisy variables, select informational variables, and group objects of similar characteristics. The spike distribution is symmetric and concentrated around zero, while the slab distribution has heavier tails to work with asymmetric data. The quantification of relevant variables is obtained by Bayes factors and encoded in a Bernoulli random variable. The procedure generates a dendrogram, a teeth plot, and a profile plot that together facilitate the visual appreciation of the different possible clusters, the relevant variables, and the optimal number of groups.

Another approach is to combine DR with CA. Regarding this, Thrun and Ultsch proposed extracting new and valid knowledge from the structures defined by a hybrid algorithm consisting of an artificial swarm (Thrun and Ultsch, 2021a) and a self-organizing map (Thrun and Ultsch, 2020b). Here, a DBS is used to find "natural" clusters based on distances and densities without imposing a particular structure on the data, unlike conventional algorithms. The coexistence of projection and clustering allows us to explore cluster structures through a topographic map without making implicit assumptions about the data (Thrun et al., 2016). The topographic map can be vividly described as a virtual 3D landscape of the data structure, with a specific color scale and level curves that visually represent the groups found in the data and the boundaries between them. Valleys and basins represent clusters, and hills and mountain ranges indicate the boundaries between clusters. These visualization-based approaches have proven their good performance in the search for structures in data (Thrun et al., 2021). The alternative to measure the error of DR methods is infeasible without prior knowledge (Thrun et al., 2023). In the following sections this will be explained in detail.

1.2.8 Semisupervised Classification

Although this Element does not address the topic of semisupervised classification (SSC) in any depth, we want to make a brief reference to it. When an archaeological investigation collects a large number of artifacts, it is not known with certainty the origin of these, so it is of interest to determine the places of supply of the raw materials. To make comparisons of the materials and find their places of origin, we make use of previous research that has already located deposits of clay, obsidian, and other geological elements. Therefore, we are dealing with the problem of partial labeling of the data. For this purpose, SSC is an efficient statistical tool that uses a large number of unlabeled samples (i.e., artifacts of unknown source) along with a smaller number of labeled samples (i.e., collected geological samples) in the learning process. In this classification scheme, an algorithm is trained using samples with known origin; once the algorithm is trained, it is used to automatically predict the class labels of unlabeled data.

Many semisupervised (SS) algorithms assume finite mixture Gaussian distributions for clustering; in the case of partial labeling, analog model-based SS clustering is used. A mixture model is a probabilistic model that represents the presence of subpopulations within a larger dataset. An example is the one published by Murphy et al. (2010), who developed a DA method based on an SS model that also includes variable selection. Similarly, Lebret et al. (2015) implemented in the package "Rmixmod" for R a method that fits Gaussian mixture models and runs in the three classification systems (unsupervised, supervised, and semisupervised). In this method, the belonging of the observations to one of the K-groups is estimated by the rule called maximum a posteriori probability (MAP), which considers the conditional probability that the observation x_i comes from group k.

The advantage of Rmixmod is that it allows the fitting of a family of twenty-eight Gaussian models that are tested on the same dataset. To choose the best of all models, the Bayesian information criterion (BIC) and CV are used. These allow us to evaluate the predictive capacity of the potential models and help determine the appropriate number of components to keep in the model. In summary, finite mixture models are more robust in situations where the origin of the sample or the group to which it belongs is completely unknown, but its membership of one of the established groups can be determined by means of a probability density function (PDF). The application of SS methods has been increasing recently in different research areas and, in the near future, promises advances in the classification of archaeological materials and provenance studies.

A more comprehensive explanation of the various model-based clustering approaches can be found in Bouveyron and Brunet-Saumard (2014), Everitt and Hand (1981), Fop and Murphy (2018), Heller (2007), and Lebret et al. (2015). For a specific application of SSC to archaeology, see López-García et al. (2024).

1.3 Last but Not Least

The final but also important step in data analysis and processing is the **validation of the results**. This essential part of the clustering/classification procedures makes it possible to objectively determine the quality and robustness of the groups found, as well as to know to what extent the modeling represents a good classification scheme. In other words, the validation criteria provide information about the quality of the clustering solutions, the degree to which a cluster method fits a specific dataset, and the ability to determine the optimal number of clusters in the partition of the dataset. A large number of investigations in archaeometry use exploratory techniques without validating the results, and it is common to observe graphs where they are presented with several degrees of overlap between data clouds or with a large dispersion of these, making it impossible to clearly identify the groups. For this reason, it is important to evaluate the result of a clustering using proper statistical methods with an acceptable level of confidence so that the inferences are the closest to reality.

To evaluate clustering analysis solutions, two approaches can be used: visualizations, like heatmaps (Wilkinson and Friendly, 2009) and topographic maps (Thrun et al., 2016), and validation measures. There are two types of validation measures: internal (i.e., without prior classification) and external (i.e., with prior classification). The first is based on external criteria that compare the results of the clustering with externally verified results, as would be the case when the researcher knows a priori some labels of the classes; an example is the Rand Index (Ball and Geyer-Schulz, 2018; Hubert and Arabie, 1985; Rand, 1971). The second is based on internal criteria that assess how good the structure of the clustering is, without the need for information outside the algorithm itself and its result; the latter fundamentally measures the homogeneity and separation of clusters, like the Davies Bouldin Index (Davies and Bouldin, 1979) and the Dunn Index (Dunn, 1974). For example, in this Element, robust validation of the models is proposed and applied, such as through silhouette statistics (Kaufman and Rousseeuw, 2005; Rousseeuw, 1987).

It is important to keep in mind that if the information presented is incorrect, the entire interpretation of the data can be compromised. On the other hand, by checking if our procedure is correct and if the data fit the model, we increase confidence in our results, and we will have a greater degree of certainty in the inferences produced. The measures are accessible in the R package "FCPS" on CRAN (https://CRAN.R-project.org/package=FCPS) published in Thrun and Stier (2021). The following sections describe, discuss, and show when to apply more robust statistical methods for processing quantitative archaeological data, in both low- and high-dimensional spaces. These methods demonstrate their good performance in the search for structures in the data without incurring errors such as overlapping or misassignment of samples to groups, regardless of the sample size or the number of variables, which is part of the weaknesses of classical multivariate methods.

2 Processing Spectral Data

One of the general goals pursued by archaeometric studies is to obtain the chemical composition of archaeological artifacts by measuring them with different instrumental methods. The amount of raw data acquired by some spectroscopic instruments, such as FT-IR, Raman spectroscopy, or XRF spectrometry, can vary from hundreds to thousands of descriptors. For example, portable XRF (pXRF) produces a large amount of data for each analyzed sample relative to the photon counts per channel division ($n \ll p$), where n represents the number of analyzed samples and p represents the channel counts (or wavelengths in other instruments). When the dimensionality of the data is high, the suggested approach is to apply a DR method to the data and then use a clustering method on the reduced space (Baxter, 2015). Under this scenario, DR techniques are essential elements for data analysis that have been and continue to be commonly used as a tool in the search for underlying structures in data.

However, classical multivariate statistical methods do not solve certain problems present in spectral data, such as collinearity and information redundancy, reducing the prediction accuracy of a statistical model. There is an alternative way to deal with the problems of high dimensionality and clustering: taking a high-dimensional model-based approach based on the use of probabilistic models for clusters and optimizing the fit between the data and the theoretical model. Model-based clustering is an approach defined in a probabilistic framework; it considers the existence of two or more subpopulations within the general population and assumes that the data of each class are generated by different probability distributions. Each probability distribution models the data of a different class with specific characteristics; the set of all distributions is modeled as the sum of the parametric distributions (Fraley and Raftery, 1998; McLachlan and Peel, 2000). Because model-based clustering is an inferential procedure, it uses model selection methods for deciding the number of components in the sample and the group membership (Papageorgiou et al., 2001; Raftery and Dean, 2006).

Post-probabilities are interpreted as measures of similarity of the new object to one of the K-classes. Model-based grouping has the advantage of not relying on a distance matrix and includes an extensive family of algorithms. Some publications that outline various approaches of model-based clustering in detail are Bouveyron and Brunet-Saumard (2014), Everitt and Hand (1981), Fop and Murphy (2018), and Heller (2007). In the context of archaeology, Litton and Buck (1995) explored the Bayesian paradigm combined with the Gibbs sampling criterion for provenance studies; Buck and Litton (1996) presented some applications for the clustering and seriation of data in which it is assumed that covariance matrices are identical in the model; and Papageorgiou and Liritzis (2007) used the iterative Bayesian technique of Reversible Jump Markov Chain Monte Carlo to classify 188 ceramic samples from Mesolithic, Neolithic, and Bronze ages.

Model-based clustering methods are categorized into (a) regularization, (b) constrained and parsimonious models, (c) subspace clustering techniques, and

(d) variable selection techniques (Bouveyron and Brunet-Saumard, 2014). We focus on the last category, (d), which is more suitable for the behavior of the data analyzed here (where $n \ll p$). This choice was based on the problem of collinearity in the spectra, in which there is a strong correlation between explanatory variables. Therefore, it is advisable to apply a variable selection method that removes variables in the context of classification because irrelevant or redundant variables could severely affect the result of the clustering algorithms.

2.1 Why Work with Full Spectra?

Archaeometric research usually works with elemental concentrations expressed as weight percent or parts per million to parts per billion. However, when converting the measurements into elemental concentrations, calibration is an important step. For example, to perform calibrations in XRF, the photon counts or peak intensities of the analytes have to be measured along with certified reference materials (CRMs) (Rousseau, 2001). Speakman (2012) suggests verifying the accuracy of a calibration by contrasting it with independent quality control standards. For the case of obsidian materials, Speakman (2012) concludes that the factory calibration (Bruker in this case) had almost a direct correspondence with the recommended values in 1 sigma, establishing its validity and reliability for elemental analyses of this type of material (Glascock and Ferguson, 2012; Speakman, 2012). Nevertheless, the situation is very different for ceramic materials.

Because ceramics are much more heterogeneous, some special considerations must be taken into account when evaluating the appropriate matrix correction procedures for instruments such as pXRF or any other spectrometric technique. One is to check the concentration ranges of the elements covered by the factory calibrations, but usually these do not adequately cover the concentration ranges found for many archaeological ceramic samples (Barwick, 2003). Hunt and Speakman (2015) emphasize that the calibration must contain all the potential elements of interest for a given material and ensure that appropriate materials and devices are used to prepare calibration standards. This also implies having a set of standards that contain a known amount of the elements of the type of analyte of interest, measuring the instrument response for each standard and establishing the relationship between the instrument response and the analyte concentration (Barwick, 2003).

In this regard, Hunt and Speakman (2015) contrast a manufacturer's recommended calibration for ceramics and soils ("mudrock") and a clay/sediment calibration developed by the Center for Applied Isotope Studies (CAIS).

Examining the calibration function, Hunt and Speakman (2015) showed that the pXRF mudrock calibration produced a relationship that is clearly not linear in all cases, which is reflected in the values calculated for the correlation coefficient R^2. The mudrock calibration also did not produce suitable results for several components, such as V, Cr, Co, or Ni. In addition, Gallhofer and Lottermoser (2018) quantified critical elements in geological materials using preinstalled factory calibration software, determining that precision of many critical elements in twenty-one CRMs is acceptable (< 20%RSD), although the accuracy can be poor (> 50% difference). Gallhofer and Lottermoser (2018) concluded that various elements might cause spectral interferences and hamper the quantification of a specific element.

Another problem is that the quality of the analytical method is highly dependent on the linearity of the calibration curve and needs to be carefully evaluated by calculating the coefficient of determination (R^2). Nevertheless, R^2 should be used with care when evaluating the linearity of calibration lines. For example, a correlation coefficient very close to 1 can also be obtained from a clearly curved relationship (Van Loco et al., 2002), even when any curvature suggests a lack of fit due to a nonlinear effect. For these cases, the residual plots give useful information for validating the chosen linear calibration model with some statistical tests, such as the Lack-of-Fit test or Mandel's fitting test.

In summary, calibration testing needs to be well designed, and the calibration standards need to adequately cover the range of concentrations found in the test samples (the standard samples should be analyzed in the same matrix as the unknown sample). To develop successful calibrations, it is critical to consider the number of standards and the number of replicates at each calibration level and then perform the relevant calibrations by a correction model (i.e., empirical correction curves, influence coefficient, fundamental parameters, or Compton normalization). It should not be forgotten that certified standards of a reference material also have uncertainties, so one recommendation is to avoid the use of commercial or automatic calibration software, as well as unprocessed intensity data (Ceccarelli et al., 2016).

Therefore, in cases where we cannot trust in factory calibrations and/or access to CMRs is complicated, it is proposed to analyze the full spectrum. The spectrum registers all the energy emitted by a sample and can be numerically expressed as a matrix; for example, XRF can be numerically expressed as the distribution of the frequencies of photon counts versus energy levels (Lopez-Garcia et al., 2019). After suitable preprocessing, the spectra can be handled by using high-dimensional model-based clustering, which models the distribution of a random sample and clusters the datasets.

2.2 Data Preprocessing

To achieve accurate results, data preprocessing is a crucial and important part of handling high-dimensional data and must be the first step in data analysis. Spectrum pretreatments reduce noise contributions, allowing the unwanted effects of the components outside the visible information to be corrected. Raw spectra must be preprocessed following three basic steps. First, the spectra are treated by extended multiplicative signal correction (EMSC) with a sixth-degree polynomial algorithm to correct noisy effects, such as light scattering due to heterogeneities of the sample (Martens and Stark, 1991). Subsequently, these data are filtered with the Savitzky–Golay algorithm, with a third-degree polynomial considering eleven points; this smooths the spectra without loss of information. If the spectral data present horizontal shifts, a peak alignment must be performed by implementing a hierarchical cluster-based peak alignment algorithm. Finally, outliers are detected with the robust principal component analysis (ROBPCA) approach, a robust version of PCA that combines projection pursuit (PP) ideas with robust scatter matrix estimation (Hubert and Engelen, 2004).

2.2.1 Extended Multiplicative Signal Correction

In addition to useful information, the collected spectra may also contain irrelevant information; preprocessing removes systematic noise and other spurious data. The EMSC method is a suitable tool for the correction of various adverse effects of the signal, such as additive baseline variation, multiplicative scaling and scatter, and interference effects (Afseth and Kohler, 2012). The EMSC implements a model-based background rectification and standardization of the spectra, eliminating identified but undesired physical interferences while retaining identified and unidentified desired effects in the data (dos Santos Panero et al., 2013). For applying this filter to the spectra, use the package "EMSC" version 0.9.2 for R published by Liland and Indahl (2020); the code is provided in *Machine Learning for Archaeological Applications in R*.

2.2.2 Savitzky–Golay Filter

Another preprocessing technique that has proven to be effective for data smoothing and noise removal is the Savitzky–Golay (SG) filter, which employs a polynomial regression method that operates as a weighted sum over a given window whose size depends on the selected polynomial order and degree (Stevens et al., 2022). It is based on a local least squares polynomial approximation that reduces the random noise of the instrumental signal without distorting the signal, that is, keeping the shape and height of the waveform peaks (Schafer, 2011). The idea of SG filtering is to find the coefficients c_n that preserve higher moments.

In the input, two design parameters must be specified: the window length and the filter order. The selection of the appropriate filter parameters influences the behavior of the filter. The window length sets the parameters $nl = nL$ (L is the number of points used "to the left"), $nr = nR$ (R is the number of points used to the right), and $m = M$ (polynomial degree). Depending on the window size, the filter will reduce the original matrix size by eliminating some values from both extremes of the data matrix or vector. To filter the spectra with the SG algorithm, use the "prospectr" package published by Stevens and Ramirez–Lopez (2015); the code is provided in *Machine Learning for Archaeological Applications in R*.

2.2.3 Peak Alignment

Certain instruments, such as pXRF, can present shifts in the horizontal axis related to energy calibration over time, possibly due to variable experimental or instrumental conditions. Therefore, it is frequent to find spectra that show small horizontal displacements in the positioning of the peaks (Wehrens, 2011), which can occur in only some segments or in the entire spectrum (Figure 10). Unnoticed misalignments of the spectra can propagate error in the analysis and give erroneous results in the classification of the data.

To correct misaligned spectra, the robust and highly consistent alignment algorithm known as hierarchical cluster-based peak alignment (CluPA) can be employed (Vu et al., 2011). All the spectra are aligned by the algorithm based on a reference spectrum and by building a hierarchical cluster tree from the reference peak lists and the target spectrum and then dividing it into predefined equivalent window-sized sections (Beirnaert et al., 2018). The package "speaq" for R environment, described in López-García et al. (2019), can be employed to align the spectra; the code is provided in *Machine Learning for Archaeological Applications in R*.

2.2.4 Outlier Detection

The third and final stage of data preprocessing is the detection of outliers. An outlier is an observation that is numerically distant from the rest of the data and can have contaminating effects on the results. Hawkins (1980) defines an outlier as an observation that deviates greatly from other observations and raises the suspicion that it was generated by a different pattern. Classic multivariate methods based on the vector of means and the covariance and correlation

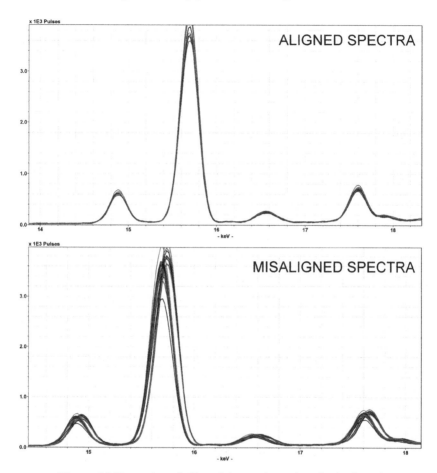

Figure 10 Examples of aligned (upper image) and misaligned
(lower image) spectra.

Note: Colour version available at www.cambridge.org/knowledge_materials.

matrices are particularly sensitive to the presence of outliers, which makes it important to identify them prior to modeling and analysis. Without an adequate diagnosis of the data, it is unlikely to obtain precise inferences that allow characterization of the process under study. Furthermore, the results may present important biases that lead to erroneous interpretations if these atypical observations are not detected in time.

One of the most widely used methods for detecting outliers is the Mahalanobis distance. However, this method, along with other distances commonly used for this purpose, undergoes adverse effects such as masking and swamping, as described in Section 1 of this Element. Masking occurs when one, or more, outlying observations biases the mean and covariance estimates toward it, or them, and the resulting distance of these outlying observations from the mean is small. Swamping occurs when multiple outliers distort the classical estimates of the sample mean and covariance in such a way that observations that are consistent with most of the data obtain larger values (Filzmoser et al., 2016). These drawbacks can be solved more effectively if the classic multivariate location and scatter estimators are replaced by robust methods that are not influenced by the presence of these observations. Robust methods have a break point of up to 0.5, which means that up to 50 percent of the data can have extreme values without affecting the estimate (Wehrens, 2011).

In cases where $n \ll p$, Hubert et al. (2005) proposed the algorithm known as ROBPCA as an efficient method for DR and outlier detection, combining ideas from both PP and robust covariance estimation. This method performs a decomposition of singular data values (SVD) to express the information in the n-dimensional space (Filzmoser and Todorov, 2011). The PP is used to preprocess the data so that the transformed data can lie in a subspace whose dimension is at most $n - 1$ (Hubert and Vanden Branden, 2003). Then, ROBPCA can find the linear combinations of the original variables that contain the most information; at the same time, it identifies outliers and determines whether they are highly contaminating or the type that does not influence the estimates.

Afterwards, the fast algorithm that calculates the minimum covariance determinant (MCD) or the fast minimum covariance determinant (FAST-MCD) is used to obtain the robust location and covariance matrix (Nurunnabi et al., 2012), which is one of the most recommended robust estimators (Rousseeuw and van Driessen, 1999). This method replaces classic covariance matrices with a robust covariance matrix obtained with the MCD method (Todorov and Filzmoser, 2009). It focuses on finding h observations (out of n) whose covariance matrix has the lowest determinant (Rousseeuw and van Driessen, 1999). An advantage of the MCD is that it can resist a large fraction of outliers ($n - h + 1$), and its influence function is bounded (Rousseeuw and Hubert, 2017). This technique maximizes a robust measure of dispersion and obtains consecutive directions in which the data points are projected (Hubert et al., 2005).

For this step, the diagnosis is performed through the MCD estimator of the package "rrcov" version 1.5-5, published by Todorov (2020); the script is provided in *Machine Learning for Archaeological Applications in R*. This algorithm returns a diagnostic plot in which each observation is projected, allowing detection and classification of potential outliers and their different types depending on their position in the robust subspace of the PCA. This graphic displays the robust distances between each of the observations: orthogonal distance versus score distance (Rousseeuw and van Zomeren, 1990).

The robust score distance (SDi) is represented on the abscissa or horizontal coordinate axis (x), while on the ordinate or vertical coordinate axis (y) are the orthogonal distances (ODi) (Verboven and Hubert, 2005).

For classifying the observations, cutoff values are set according to Hubert et al. (2005), who propose two thresholds that are viewed as vertical and horizontal lines that intersect. The x-axis threshold is determined by $\sqrt{X^2_{k,0.975}}$ when $k > 1$ and $\pm \sqrt{X^2_{k,0.975}}$ when $k = 1$, assuming that the squared distances of the Mahalanobis distance are distributed as X^2_k. The threshold for the y-axis is obtained through the Wilson–Hilferty approximation, which is a scaled version of the $g1X^2_{g2}$ distribution ($\tilde{\mu} + \sigma_{z,0.975^{3/2}}$) with $z_{0.975} = \Phi^{-1}(0.975)$ that corresponds to the 97.5% quartile (1.96 value) of the normal distribution (Engelen and Hubert, 2004; Hubert et al., 2005; Varmuza and Filzmoser, 2009; Verboven and Hubert, 2005). Points beyond both thresholds, that is, whose distances are greater than the cutoff value in the x- and y-axes, are considered outliers. By plotting ODi and SDi along with two thresholds or cutoff values set for the outlier designation, the observations can be classified into four different types of outliers (Figure 11).

The observations that fall in the first quadrant ("regular observations") are uniformly distributed in the PCA space and do not represent any problem. The observations that are projected in the upper-left quadrant are called "orthogonal outliers" and correspond to observations that are not visible when the data are projected in a 2D graph of the PCA space; these observations can alter the results in the classic PCA. Observations in the upper-right quadrant record high values of both ODi and SDi ("bad leverage points") and can force the estimation

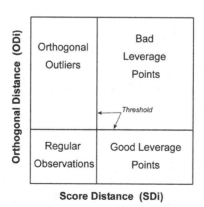

Figure 11 Distance–distance map of the ROBPCA method.

Note: Colour version available at www.cambridge.org/knowledge_materials.

of the PCA space. Those observations whose distances are greater than the X^2 threshold are marked as atypical observations. It is recommended not to ignore or just delete these observations as they may contain important information or come from another population, statistically speaking. Finally, the observations that record a high value of SDI but with a small ODi ("good leverage points") have no impact on the estimates and can even stabilize the estimate in the PCA space (Varmuza and Filzmoser, 2009).

2.3 Model-Based Approach for Variable Selection, Classification, and Clustering

After the preprocessing of the data has been concluded, we can employ classification methods. In high-dimensional data, it is not necessary to include all the variables in the analysis to discriminate groups, as the inherent structure of grouping observations can be contained in a small subset of optimal variables and not all of the p-variables contribute to the correct classification of the data (Tadesse et al., 2005). It is important to note that the inclusion of noninformative variables ("*masking*" variables) can "hide" the true cluster structure, drastically affecting the result of the clustering algorithms (Grün, 2019). Moreover, the exclusion of important variables from the model can also generate incorrect interpretations of the real structure of the data. This can be reflected in the poor estimation of the number of clusters, as well as the erroneous assignment of the instances to the groups (Wang and Zhu, 2008).

In contrast, the retention of potentially optimal variables in a model can result in the identification of clusters having a more direct correspondence with the true underlying group structure (Raftery and Dean, 2006). Model-based CA can specify the role of each variable (Maugis et al., 2009). This method divides the set of variables into a subset of relevant clustering variables and a subset of irrelevant variables, considering that some of the irrelevant variables can be dependent or independent of the relevant clustering variables. In the context of model-based clustering, Partovi Nia and Davison (2012) propose a Bayesian model-based approach known as the "spike-and-slab" mixture model; it is based on a combination of two continuous distributions with zero mean and different variances. An example of a spike-and-slab distribution is shown in Figure 12.

The terms spike and slab are typically used for a distribution that models knowledge a priori. This model allows for variable selection, clustering, and classification in a single setting, separating the variables into two groups: one consisting of important and influential variables for the clustering task and a second group of variables with insignificant effects; an additional advantage

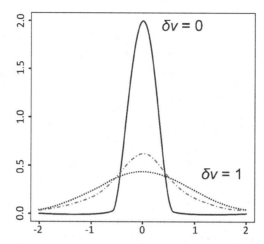

Figure 12 Example of Gaussian spike (solid line) and slab (dotted
and dashed lines) distributions.

Note: Colour version available at www.cambridge.org/knowledge_materials.

of this algorithm is that it automatically determines the optimal number of
clusters in the data. Mixture priors with spike-and-slab components have been
used extensively for variable selection in linear regression problems (see
George and McCulloch, 1993, 1997; Mitchell and Beauchamp, 1988). The
model considers the systematic variation of the spectra readings of the analytes
to determine those variables that potentially contribute the most to the clustering
task. The aim is to group the archaeological samples into disjoint classes based
on the measured variables to debug all those variables that turn out to be
nonsignificant.

To use this distribution to select variable-class combinations, it is necessary
to enter a discrete (Bernoulli) or indicator variable (δv) into the model to
control the inclusion and exclusion of the variable-class effect with probabilities p and q, respectively. This allows selection of the most relevant variables
for clustering. If the variables are assigned to the slab component of the *prior*,
the indicator variable has a value of $\delta v = 1$. Then, the variable-class combination is active. Otherwise, if $\delta v = 0$, the variable-class combination is inactive
and corresponds to the spike distribution. The variable-class combination
follows the scale proposed by Kass and Raftery (1995). Regarding this,
Partovi Nia and Davison (2012) established a scale of interpretation of the
Bayes factor B_v: clearly important ($\log B_v > 5$), important ($3 < \log B_v \leq 5$),
somewhat important ($1 < \log B_v \leq 3$), and negligible ($0 < \log B_v \leq 1$); negative
values of $\log B_v$ are unimportant.

Fitting the model requires specification of the distribution family. To calculate the mixture prior, two distributions are used: Gaussian and asymmetric Laplace distributions. The second is used to model asymmetric distributions with heavier tails; the two distributions are centered at zero. In the proposed model, the marginal distribution has an analytically closed form (Partovi Nia and Davison, 2012). The log Bayes factor B_δ evaluates the importance of variables, and the factor $B\gamma$ measures the importance of the variable-cluster combination (Fop and Murphy, 2018). The model assumes that all combinations of variable-class are independent, thereby ignoring the correlations between variables. It also assumes that the data have been centered. For this, the data must be transformed into a *Z score* $(0,1)$ before the analysis so that the averages are equal to zero.

The hyperparameters of the prior density are estimated from the data by maximizing the likelihood function under a fully marginal model. In the original version of this algorithm, it is possible to work with replicas made on an experimental unit or considering each individual case without replication. In the unreplicated clustering, the Gaussian model has six parameters (φ): $\log \sigma_\varepsilon^2$, $\log \sigma_\eta^2$, $\log \sigma_\theta^2$, μ, logit p, and logit q, where σ^2 is the replicate error variance, σ_η^2 is the variance of between-type error, σ_θ^2 is the variance of the disappearing random component, μ is the general level, p is the proportion of active variable-class combinations, and q is the proportion of the active variables (Partovi Nia and Davison, 2015). In the last step, the method performs bottom-up hierarchical clustering to find the maximum clustering posterior, assuming a multinomial-Dirichlet distribution (objective function) as the allocation prior.

Based on a monotone height function, it generates a dendrogram based on the marginal posterior probabilities. The log posterior is used as a natural distance imposed by the model to construct the hierarchical tree. The method initializes each data point as a single cluster and iteratively merges pairs of clusters that maximize the clustering posterior. This merging process is repeated until the assignment of the observations is complete and all groups have been formed. The posterior-based dendrogram has a probabilistic interpretation for the output data, indicating which is the best clustering under the model. The optimal clustering is found by cutting the dendrogram with the maximum a posteriori clustering principle (Partovi Nia and Davison, 2015). More detailed information about Bayesian hierarchical clustering using spike-and-slab models can be found in Partovi Nia and Davison (2012).

To apply the Bayesian approach to cluster the data using spike-and-slab models, with priors for model parameters and for the allocation of subjects to groups, we ran the package "bclust" version 2.15.0 for R published by

Partovi Nia and Davison (2015). The related script can be consulted in *Machine Learning for Archaeological Applications in R*.

3 Processing Compositional Data

The postulate of provenance of Weigand et al. (1977) establishes that artifacts originating from the same source of raw material present lower variability than those existing between different sources. The variability is associated with different discrete units or geographic areas. Therefore, it is logical to think that if a suitable classification method is used, it should be possible to partition the analyzed samples into natural clusters that can be differentiated from other clusters according to their characteristics. Therefore, it should be possible to correctly assign artifacts of unknown origin to their respective natural sources. Accordingly, the clusters formed must be cohesive and well separated from other data (Baudry et al., 2010) and not clusters with overlapping, scattered, or sparsely separated data points. Regarding the studies conducted with obsidian artifacts, this postulate is easier to fulfill because the chemical composition of the individual geological sources is quite homogeneous.

Conversely, in ceramic studies, the situation is much more complex due to the heterogeneity of the material generated by different factors: the exploitation of different clay banks, the addition of various types of temper, and the alteration of the chemical and physical components of the pieces related to the firing process. This can cause observations to be detected with multiple possible assignments (i.e., forming overlapping groups). These two cases can be related to two types of clustering. The first is crisp clustering, in which each data point belongs or does not belong to a specific cluster (clusters do not overlap). The second is fuzzy clustering, where each of the elements has a certain degree of belonging to the groups and not just one. The latter is part of the model-based clustering, which assigns maximum a posteriori cluster membership. This last approach is proposed in this section for the adequate classification of compositional data. For proper classification, several theoretical assumptions and analytical steps must be considered, which are explained here.

3.1 Defining Compositional and Completely Compositional Data

The data obtained in archaeometric analyses have a compositional character, that is, they quantitatively describe the parts that form a whole (Egozcue and Pawlowsky-Glahn, 2011). Symbolically, compositional data are represented as $x = (x_1, x_2, \ldots x_D)$ with D-parts. All the values of these vectors are positive, and the sum of all the parts will always be a constant k. If $k = 1$, it is about proportions; if $k = 100$, it is about percentages; and if $k = 1 \times 10^{-6}$, it is in parts per million (ppm). The nonnegativity and constant sum constraints that characterize this type of data imply that the multivariate techniques commonly used are not suitable for its analysis and modeling. The differences in the processing of this type of data establish following a different methodology for its correct interpretation.

In a 2002 publication, John Aitchison along with other academics appealed to those who were conducting studies in archaeometry to consider the underlying and necessary principles of the analysis of compositional data and to avoid the risk of arriving at erroneous interpretations when using standard statistical methods (Aitchison et al., 2002). This stems from the fact that the sample space of compositional data is a restricted space, and its geometry is different from the Euclidean geometry of the real space. For the case of compositional data, the simplex (S^D) is established as the sample space. It is a closed space, different from the real Euclidean space associated with unconstrained data. The simplex is explained as follows (Equation 1):

$$S^D = \left\{ \mathbf{x} = [x_1, x_2, \ldots, x_D] \mid x_i > 0, i = 1, 2, \ldots, D ; \sum_{i=1}^{D} x_1 = K \right\} \qquad (1)$$

Due to this definition, compositional data are subject to the restriction that the sum vector of the D-parts can only include values of the first octant of the Cartesian coordinate plane, unlike data that are free to vary in the real space of Euclidean geometry (Pawlosky-Glahn and Egozcue, 2006). As a general rule, when dealing with compositional data, first express the data in terms of components of *log*-ratios and then apply the appropriate multivariate methodology for unconstrained data vectors, which would now be in the real space and free from the constant sum constraint (Aitchison, 1986; Reyment and Savazzi, 1999).

The term "completely compositional" can be expressed as $\sum_i x_{ij} = k$, where k is the required sum value. If the data do not sum k, then they are known as subcompositions. These subcompositions can be normalized and treated as completely compositional by adding a residual variable (Baxter, 1995) that can be estimated from $[100 - \sum_i x_{ij}]$ for the case of percentages. Another way is to perform the closure operator (Equation 2; López-García et al., 2018):

$$C(\mathbf{x}) = \left(kx_1 / \sum x_i, \ldots, kx_D / \sum x_i \right) \qquad (2)$$

which transforms each vector of parts D into a vector that sums the whole unit managed (k). By performing either of these two operations, completely compositional data can be assumed and, consequently, transformed to suit the proper space geometry. Log-ratio methods can lead to consistent results either by working with normalized data or by adding a residual variable that completes the sum k (Pawlowsky-Glann and Egozcue, 2006).

Revelation of the cluster structure in the data depends on the choice of different strategies: the representation, transformation, and/or standardization of the data, a model-based clustering that characterizes the degree of agreement of the observations, and the selection of the optimal number of clusters. Regarding this, different studies (Baxter, 2003; Jajuga and Walesiak, 2000; Milligan and Cooper, 1988) have described the effect caused by transformation/standardization in the conservation of the structure and quality of a cluster in various data configurations. Aitchison (1986) showed that the effects of the constant sum constraint on the covariance and correlation matrices disappear if the original data are expressed as ratios of logarithms. Log-ratio methods can lead to consistent results either by working with normalized data or by adding a residual variable that completes the sum k (Pawlowsky-Glann and Egozcue, 2006).

For compositional data, three transformations are proposed: the additive log-ratio (*alr*), the centered log-ratio (*clr*), and the isometric log-ratio (*ilr*) (Aitchison, 1986; Egozcue et al., 2003). Our recommendation for processing compositional data is to use the *ilr* transformation because *alr* and *clr* present problems such as lack of symmetry and singularity, respectively (Palarea-Albaladejo et al., 2007). The *ilr* transformation is based on a sequential binary partition (SBP) of a composition of *D*-parts in nonoverlapping groups, producing compositions that are represented in Cartesian coordinates (Mateu-Figueras and Daunis-i-Estadella, 2008). It is characterized by the relative transformation of angles and distances in the simplex to angles and distances in the real space (Egozcue et al., 2003), enabling the representation of compositional data in coordinates of an orthonormal basis. In other words, the *ilr* transformation transfers the geometry of the simplex to a real multivariate space.

The *ilr* coordinate is defined as the logarithm of the ratio of the geometric means between partitions of the data matrix called balances (Egozcue and Pawlowsky-Glahn, 2005). The balances are known as log-contrasts, that is, log-ratios of the geometric mean of two nonoverlapping groups that are normalized in such a way that they become coordinates of the composition with respect to a unitary vector or balance element (Egozcue et al., 2003; Pawlowsky-Glahn and Egozcue, 2011). Balances represent elements of the simplex in the orthonormal basis defined by an SBP; each row in the SBP defines a balance of the components in the columns. Considering all the available parts in the SBP, these are divided into two groups; then, one of these groups is divided again into two groups. This procedure continues until all the formed groups contain only one part (van den Boogaart and Tolosana-Delgado, 2013).

The major advantage of the balances for the interpretation of the results is that they describe the relative behavior between the groups of parts

(Pawlowsky-Glahn and Egozcue, 2006). One option is to define an SBP of the composition (Egozcue and PawlowskyGlahn, 2005; Pawlowsky-Glahn and Egozcue, 2011). This sequence of distribution of parts can be based on our knowledge of the nature of the data. If we do not have adequate knowledge of how to define a sequential partition, Pawlowsky-Glahn and Egozcue (2011) suggest using the variation matrix or the compositional biplot as an alternative, while van den Boogaart and Tolosana-Delgado (2013) consider applying a variable clustering technique and deriving the partition structure from the resulting tree.

A simpler alternative whichs to generate the SBP automatically in R,whichch corresponds to the approximation that we follow in this application. The result of this grouping can be displayed graphically with some descriptive statistics (Martín-Fernández et al., 2015). The CoDa-dendogram is the graphic representation of the SBP that hierarchically shows how the various parts are grouped. This includes a summary of the descriptive statistics of the balances (Pawlowsky-Glahn and Egozcue, 2011), as well as the *ilr* decomposition of the total variance, the geometric mean, and the dispersion coordinates (Martín-Fernández et al., 2015). The boxplots closest to a part (or group) indicate that this part (or group) is more abundant. Another characteristic that is easily read in a CoDa-dendrogram is symmetry; it can be evaluated by comparing the boxplots or the different quantiles and observing the difference between the medians.

3.2 Standardization/Normalization

In archaeometric studies, it is a very common practice to transform the original data to $\log_{10}$ instead of standardizing it to make comparisons between sets of elements. The argument is based on two reasons; the first is that, in most cases and especially for trace elements, the distribution of the data is closer to normal. The second is that it is useful for compensating for the differences in magnitude between minor elements and trace elements (Glascock and Neff, 2003). Although the last condition can be met on certain occasions, the assumption of normality is barely satisfied in practice. It has been proven that this type of transformation does not guarantee normality and that, in most cases, the resultant distributions are not symmetrical (Filzmoser et al., 2009).

On the other hand, it is also common to find research that prefers the use of Z score (0,1) standardization [$x \leftarrow \frac{x-\mu}{\sigma}$], which refers to a transformation that results in variables with zero mean and unit variance (Baxter, 2015). The Z score can present problems if the data are contaminated with outliers. Another problem, as Grün (2019) points out, is that there are situations in which the cluster structure is not equally strong in all dimensions, and dissimilarities containing strong cluster structures can reduce the effectiveness and spoil the clustering procedure. According to Ben-Hur and Guyon (2003), standardization is recommended only when the registered variables are in different scales of measurement; if the data are in the same units, this transformation can reduce the quality of a clustering. Furthermore, Milligan and Cooper (1988) were able to determine that the Z score was the least effective in many other situations. It is important to observe that the geometric space of compositional data is the simplex.

Therefore, transforming the data with $\log_{10}$ or Z score is not justified because their native space is different. Although the *ilr* transformation produces compositional data on an orthonormal basis, it is a change of basis that is expressed as a new set of variables, some of which can present a greater variability in the scale of the observed values. Considering this concern, it is advisable to use another type of normalization to compensate for differences in magnitude and in weight of the variances observed in the input variables (Milligan and Cooper, 1988). The minimum/maximum normalization transforms the values of a variable with robust estimates $[x \leftarrow \frac{x - \text{median}(x)}{\max(x) - \min(x)}]$ for minimum $[min(x)]$ and maximum $[max(x)]$ values. This is suitable when the empirical distribution of the variables deviates from normality. Standardizing the variables using the range as a divisor gives a consistently superior recovery of the underlying structure in the data (Milligan and Cooper, 1988) and, unlike other classical standardization procedures, prevents some features from ruling over the results of a grouping or classification.

3.3 Model-Based Clustering

In Section 1, it was emphasized that classic clustering methods impose a predefined geometric shape on the data to be grouped and, therefore, were not recommended for data with distribution patterns that behave differently from those contained in the clustering algorithms. In this section, we address the clustering problem with a category of models that differs from classical methods. Model-based clustering is the general name for finite mixture model clustering for continuous data. The mixture model classifies objects that are similar to each other according to their characteristics, regardless of their number, size, or orientation. In this type of clustering, a PDF is imposed on the data represented by a finite mixture of normal distributions with parameters $ck = (\mu_k, \sum k)$, where μ_k represents the mean vector, $\sum k$ is the covariance matrix of component k, and each mixture component corresponds to a different cluster.

Model-based clustering is a defined approach for representing a PDF. Unlike distance-based methods, model-based clustering can estimate a measure of association called the posterior probability of each observation, which determines the membership of each group based on a formal probability framework (Biernacki et al., 2000). In this context, it is necessary to formulate a probabilistic model under the assumption that the data are made of K components and the empirical distribution of the data can be modeled by invoking a theoretical distribution, which is generally the normal multivariate. Each probability distribution models the data of a class and corresponds to a different cluster with specific characteristics. The set of all distributions is modeled as the sum of the parametric distributions (Fraley and Raftery, 1998; McLachlan and Peel, 2000).

This procedure uses several criteria to optimize the fit between the data and the theoretical model. Because model-based clustering is an inferential procedure, it can use model selection methods to find the number of components in the sample and the group membership (Papageorgiou et al., 2001; Raftery and Dean, 2006). Moreover, mixture models have the advantage of not relying on the distance matrix. Instead, the posterior probabilities are interpreted as a measure of similarity of the new object to one of the K-classes. The estimation of the mixture parameters is performed through maximization of the log-likelihood (ML) using the EM algorithm and EM-like algorithms.

The principle of the EM algorithm is to introduce an indicator variable that identifies the membership of a cluster of each observation in the dataset. In the case of Gaussian mixtures, the maximum likelihood solution generates a set of labels $z = \{z_1, \ldots, z_n\}$, with $z_i = (z_{i1}, \ldots, z_{iK}), z_{ik} = 1$ or 0, depending on whether x_i corresponds to the k-th mixture component or not (Fraley and Raftery, 1998). Once the mixture of multivariate normal distributions has been modeled on the empirical data, the model allows use of the MAP rule for the case of samples z_i that are completely unknown. The MAP rule consists of assigning each x_i in x^u to the component k, providing the highest conditional probability that x_i arises from it (Biernacki et al., 2006). In this way, each of the observations can be assigned to each of the G-groups.

The more suitable models, each one defined by a mixture of different components that can be Gaussian or non-Gaussian, are selected according to the principle of parsimony and considering the parameterization of the covariance matrix $\sum k$ in terms of its eigenvalue decomposition:

$$\sum_k = \lambda_k D_k A_k D_k \tag{3}$$

where $\sum k$ can be any nonsingular covariance matrix, the parameter λ_k determines the volume of the k-th cluster, D_k is its orientation, and A_k is its shape (Lebret et al., 2015). By exchanging the parameters of Equation (3), different solutions can be obtained in the clustering modeling. For the automatic selection of the model and the number of components, several information criteria help in the selection of the best solution. These are the BIC, the integrated complete likelihood (ICL), and the normalized entropy criterion (NEC). A more comprehensive explanation of the various model-based clustering approaches can be found in Bouveyron and Brunet-Saumard (2014), Everitt and Hand (1981), Fop and Murphy (2018), and Heller (2007).

In the literature, we can also find many algorithms dedicated to the estimation of mixture models. Among some of the most cited are EMCluster (Chen and Maitra, 2019), mixtools (Benaglia et al., 2009), bgmm (Biecek et al., 2012), mclust (Fraley et al., 2012), MoEClust (Murphy and Murphy, 2020), and Rmixmod (Lebret et al., 2015). To reveal the clustering structure of the data, we recommend the use of two packages whose underlying theory is model-based clustering: *Rmixmod* and *ClusVis*. The *Rmixmod* package (Lebret et al., 2015) is a powerful tool for density estimation, CA, and discriminant analysis. On the other hand, the *ClusVis* package (Biernacki et al., 2019) allows visualization of the model-based clustering resulting from the previous package based on the probabilities of the classification.

Rmixmod provides an unsupervised model-based clustering method that discovers significant groups while automatically assigning observations to groups, allowing overcoming the deficiencies presented in the calculation of the probabilities with Mahalanobis distance (used to obtain the group membership of the observations). This package was primarily intended to perform clustering tasks using mixture modeling, but it also contains routines for performing supervised and semisupervised analyses; for continuous variables, up to twenty-eight multivariate Gaussian mixture models can be adjusted (Lebret et al., 2015). For estimating the mixture parameters, there are three different algorithms: EM, stochastic EM (SEM), and classification EM (CEM). These three algorithms can be initialized in different ways, leading to different strategies in the clustering task (Biernacki et al., 2006). The selection of the model among a finite set of models is established using the BIC, ICL, and NEC criteria.

Additionally, the *ClusVis* package is a generic method for visualizing the results of a model-based clustering computed from the probabilities of the conditional classification membership. The algorithm projects the data onto R^2 based on a spherical Gaussian mixture (g) with the same number of components as the native grouping mixture (f), preserving as much as possible the separation of the components obtained from the original modeling (Biernacki et al., 2021). In other words, the algorithm matches any clustering mixture and a spherical multivariate Gaussian visualization mixture according to the intersection of its components. To represent the distribution on its most discriminatory map, an LDA is applied using the eigenvalue decomposition of the covariance matrix $\sum_k$, computed on the centers μ by considering the mixture proportions π_k (Biernacki et al, 2019).

The resulting bivariate spherical Gaussian plot will be associated with the confidence areas of the components. In this type of plot, the 95% confidence level will be delimited by a black border that separates the area outside the confidence level (in white) from the area inside the confidence level (in gray levels) with $\alpha = 0.05$ (Biernacki et al., 2021). The percentage of inertia by axis can be used as a measure of the discriminant power of the mapping. The closer the sum of the first two dimensions is to 100%, the better. The quality of the mapping in the final mixture space (g), compared to the mapping of the mixture in the native space (f), is measured through the difference in the normalized entropy (f, g). The range of values of $\delta_E(f, \hat{g})$ goes from $[-1, 0, 1]$, with the value of $\delta_E(f, \hat{g}) = 0$ being the most accurate in terms of mapping accuracy between the overlapping of the components f and g. The related scripts for R, as well as examples of the application of the proposed methods to real archaeological data, can be consulted in *Machine Learning for Archaeological Applications in R*.

4 Processing a Combination of Spectral and Compositional Data

When working directly with the spectra, there are several things that need to be considered. First, the collected spectra are usually contaminated with noise. This noise can be generated by the instrument, by the acquisition mode, or even by the sample itself, and it is necessary to decrease or eliminate it without destroying the structure of the data. Therefore, several filters can be applied; proper preprocessing can facilitate the extraction of information. Second, it is important to transform or standardize the data to avoid undesirable emphasis on variables with large variances or multimodalities (Jain and Dubes, 1988; Mörchen, 2006). Third, decorrelation is necessary because, otherwise, highly correlated features will be overweighed in the CA (Jain and Dubes, 1988).

On the other hand, a spectrogram contains a large number of variables, not all of which contain information that is relevant to the clustering task. Interval selection consists of modeling the relationship between measurements that include a large number of variables ($n \ll p$) using a calibration model that combines spectral data (x) and the chemical concentration of a single variable, used as a response variable (y), to find the best interval explaining the information. One of the most suitable approaches for selecting intervals is the iPLS method, proposed by Nørgaard et al. (2000).

Recently, a new theory was proposed that suggests the selection of an appropriate distance metric based on the multimodality of the distance distribution (Thrun, 2021b). Here, we employed the DBS method (Thrun and Ultsch, 2021a), which allows the selection of specific distance measures for a dataset. This section addresses the classification of archaeological samples by combining spectral preprocessing techniques (such as those described in Section 2), variable selection methods, and projection-based CA. The procedure is described step by step in Sections 4.1–4.4. Although the preprocessing techniques were described in Section 2, they will be briefly summarized again here.

4.1 Preprocessing the Spectra

When analyzing our materials, in addition to useful information, the collected spectra may contain irrelevant information and noise. For example, spectroscopic techniques such as pXRF can cause scattering effects due to the physical characteristics of the sample, such as the roughness of the surface of obsidian samples or ceramic pastes. These issues can have an impact on qualitative and quantitative analyses. Spectra are often preprocessed to remove systematic "noise" and other spurious data. In practice, it is common to use a variety of preprocessing techniques and their combinations to obtain a model with greater predictive abilities and enhance the quality of the signal specificity. In the literature, there are many signal correction algorithms that are used to filter noise from the spectrum matrix system, such as the background signal (Wehrens, 2011) and light scattering (Lu et al., 2006; Martens and Stark, 1991; Martens et al., 2003; Savitzky and Golay, 1964).

A particular type of low-pass filter is the SG filter, which employs a method for data smoothing and noise removal. This filter reduces any random noise of the instrumental signal while preserving the characteristics of the initial distribution, the relative maxima and minima, and the width between peaks (Schafer, 2011). Another preprocessing technique for spectral filtering is the EMSC method, which has proven to be a reliable tool for the correction of additive baseline, multiplicative scaling, and interference effects (Afseth and Kohler, 2012). As explained in Section 2, the EMSC performs model-based background correction and normalization of the spectra, removing identified but undesired physical and chemical interference effects while retaining identified but desired effects as well as unidentified effects in the data (dos Santos Panero et al., 2013).

In the literature, it is common to use these filters separately or in combination. In the methodology advised here, the spectra are filtered with these filters in four ways, obtaining four different matrices that are compared and evaluated at the end. The first matrix consists of the data filtered only with the SG algorithm; the second matrix involves the spectra filtered only with the EMSC algorithm; the third and fourth matrices concern a combination of both algorithms, applying the SG filter first and then the EMSC, and vice versa. These four filtering systems are processed separately with the variable selection algorithm (described in the following paragraphs) to determine which of them provides the best fit for the model according to the computed iPLS parameters. Finally, if the peaks of the spectra exhibit displacements in their horizontal position, a peak alignment should be performed via the CluPa algorithm, previously defined in Section 2.

4.2 Variable Selection: Interval Partial Least Squares

Theoretically and experimentally speaking, chemometric applications have shown that it is better to work with interval selection methods instead of managing the whole spectrum. This has resulted in the extensive use of multivariate calibration methods. Multivariate calibration is devoted to the establishment of calibration models that relate variables to the properties of interest, such as concentration values (Wang et al., 2018). One of the reasons for operating with spectral range selection methods is that spectroscopic analyses can generate numerous variables (e.g., 2047 channel count intervals in pXRF) against a small number of samples. Such high-dimensional data can lead to the "curse of dimensionality" (Bellman, 1961; Verleysen et al., 2003) or flat matrices (Wehrens, 2011) that many traditional statistical methods cannot deal with (Wang et al., 2018).

Spectral data contain a high degree of covariance and a large amount of redundant information (Nørgaard et al., 2000). The selection of specific spectral regions or variables is key to decreasing the complexity of the calibration model and increasing its predictive precision (Leardi, 2000; Nørgaard et al., 2000). The problem is to extract a subset of variables from a large set of explanatory variables associated with one quantitative response variable. Therefore, it is advisable to develop a robust calibration model with high prediction performance for selecting those variables that contain only relevant information for the target variables (Islam et al., 2018). Variable selection techniques can be used to improve chemometric models and to enhance spectral features. Here, iPLS is introduced to find the variable intervals that deliver the lowest prediction error in comparison to the full-spectrum model. In this way, the response or dependent variable (y) is employed to set up a calibration model that allows the reduction of dimensionality by eliminating all predictor variables (X) that present a high correlation or multicollinearity.

In the iPLS model, the spectral dataset is divided into intervals of equal length, resulting in a continuum of nonoverlapping subintervals in which the partial least squares (PLS) models are established (Wang et al., 2018). The PLS regression technique reduces predictors to a smaller set of uncorrelated components and performs least squares regression on these components, rather than on the original data, by relating (y) = [e.g., chemical concentration of a single element in all the samples] to (X) = [e.g., spectral data measured from the samples]. In PLS, the matrix (X) is transformed into orthogonal factors, which are linear combinations of the original variables. This operation relates each data point with a score and each component (variable) with a loading value. Therefore, there is a DR obtaining a set with a smaller number of intermediate linear latent variables that has the maximum covariance between the scores and the modeled property (Varmuza and Filzmoser, 2009).

Because the covariance is the product of the correlation between the scores and the variance of each score, these three measures are collectively maximized. The new variables are then used to perform an ordinary least squares (OLS) regression with the response variable (y). Using a procedure called peeling or deflation, the variance information of the component is removed from the (X) data. This results in a residual matrix whose dimensionality is equal to the number of original variables in (X), but the intrinsic dimensionality is reduced by one (Varmuza and Filzmoser, 2009). Once the residual matrix has been obtained, the next PLS component can be derived by maximizing the covariance between the scores and (y) again; this procedure continues iteratively until no improvement is achieved in the modeling of (y) (Varmuza and Filzmoser, 2009).

For example, if the method was applied to XRF data, the explanatory variables in the model (X) will consist of the photon counts in each of the XRF spectrum channels, and the response variable (y) will comprise the logratio transformed concentration values of a representative chemical element (e.g., strontium) measured for each of the samples. It is important to remember that the concentrations of one or a few chemical elements are considered subcompositional in nature because only a subset of components (D-parts) are used in the measurement. In this way, before opening the data, the rows of the data matrix must be rescaled to sum 100% by applying the closure operator (Equation 4):

$$Cx = \frac{kx_1}{\sum_{i=1}^{D} x_i}, \frac{kx_2}{\sum_{i=1}^{D} x_i}, \dots, \frac{kx_D}{\sum_{i=1}^{D} x_i} \qquad (4)$$

Afterwards, we can work with any of the transformations for compositional data, all of which are based on log-ratios between the parts of compositional data. See Section 3 for revising the theory related to compositional data analysis. In this scenario, we recommend using the *clr* due to its one-to-one relationship between the original *D*-parts and the transformed variables. In other words, if you have ten input variables, the *clr* transformation will return ten output variables. This transformation is estimated through Equation 5:

$$v = clr(x) = ln \frac{x_1}{g_m(x)}, \frac{x_2}{g_m(x)}, \dots, \frac{x_D}{g_m(x)} \qquad (5)$$

where $g_m(x)$ represents the geometric mean.

The selected variable (y) is saved in a separate file as a data vector and the matrix (X), with the photon counts in each of the channel intervals in another file. In this way, the data are prepared to be processed with the iPLS method. The main contribution of the iPLS is to provide a general image of the significant information in the different spectral subdivisions, ordering the different sub-intervals according to their importance and discarding the regions without any apparent contribution (Nørgaard et al., 2000). This is achieved by comparing the global PLS model (full spectrum) and the prediction performance of the local PLS models for each subinterval.

The best subintervals are decided based on the squared correlation coefficient (r^2), which goes from −1 to 1, and the root mean squared error of CV (RMSECV), with a range of values between 0 and 1 (Islam et al., 2018), choosing the region with the lowest RMSECV. The RMSECV is considered an excellent general-purpose error metric for numerical predictions and a good measure of precision. Other parameters are also used to select the best interval and for model evaluation, such as the root mean squared error of prediction (RMSEP), which is an estimate of the prediction error (Nørgaard et al., 2000). For example, a good calibration model should have a high r^2 coefficient (nearer to 1) and a low RMSECV and RMSEP (closer to 0); if the difference between the RMSECV and the RMSEP is small, the model is considered more robust.

An additional advantage of this method is that it allows selecting the optimal spectral interval for establishing the number of latent variables (LVs) or components to retain. For more details about the method, we refer the reader to Nørgaard et al. (2000). The iPLS calibration model can be performed with the package "mdatools" for R (Kucheryavskiy, 2020). In "mdatools," you can run iPLS selection using function "ipls()"; the matrices with the predictors (X) and the response variable (y) are specified, and a model (m) is created where the intervals in the vector (already selected) are combined. The script can be consulted in *Machine Learning for Archaeological Applications in R*.

4.3 Introduction to the Use of Projection-Based Clustering

We can describe CA as the identification of high-dimensional distances and density-based structures in data. There is no precise general framework for such structure detection; it is more of an art that often requires experienced data scientists to perform. For example, currently, there are more than fifty clustering algorithms available (Thrun and Stier, 2021), and even the definition of a cluster remains the topic of scientific discussion (Bonner, 1964; Estivill-Castro, 2002; Hennig et al., 2015). The next two challenges we face are to know whether cluster structures exist (Thrun, 2020) and how many partitions there are prior to the CA (see review in Thrun, 2021a). We can use statistical testing for the existence of cluster structures (Adolfsson et al., 2019) and apply one of more than twenty indices that indicate the number of (possible) partitions in the data (Thrun and Stier, 2021). Either way, the clustering solution should always be evaluated. That said, quality measures are biased (Ball and Geyer-Schulz, 2018; Handl et al., 2005; Thrun, 2021a) and, hence, require prior assumptions about the data.

One solution for these challenges is to propose an approach in which DR methods coexist with clustering algorithms (Thrun and Ultsch, 2021b). Using DR techniques reduces the input space's dimensions to facilitate the exploration of structures in high-dimensional data. Two general DR approaches exist: manifold learning and projection methods (Venna et al., 2010). Manifold learning methods attempt to find a subspace in which the high-dimensional distances can be preserved. These subspaces may have a dimensionality of greater than two. However, only 2D or 3D representations of high-dimensional data are easily grasped for the human observer. "Manifold learning methods are not necessarily good for ... visualization ... since they have been designed to find a manifold, not compress it into a lower dimensionality" (Venna et al., 2010: 452), and van der Maaten et al. (2009) showed that they do not outperform classical PCA for real-world tasks.

Projection-based clustering (PBC) uses methods that project data explicitly into two dimensions disregarding the subspaces, but it only tries to preserve ("relevant") neighborhoods. This means that the projection methods used in PBC try to lose information which they disregard as irrelevant. To accomplish this, projection methods most often use nonlinear combinations of dimensions through an annealing scheme and neighborhoods (e.g., Demartines and Hérault, 1995; Thrun and Ultsch, 2021a; Ultsch, 1995; Venna et al., 2010) to entangle complex clusters such as two intertwined chains (see Thrun and Ultsch, 2020b). Using PBC requires following three steps, as follows (Thrun, 2022).

Let d-dimensional data points $i \in I$ be in the input space $I \subset \mathbb{R}^d$, and let $o \in O$ be projected points in the output space $O \subset \mathbb{R}^b$, then a mapping proj: $I \rightarrow O, i \mapsto o$ is called a projection if $b = 2$. First, a nonlinear projection (e.g., via NeRV [Venna et al., 2010], t-SNE [van der Maaten and Hinton, 2008], Pswarm [Thrun and Ultsch, 2021a]) is computed for the data points. Second, the projection points are quantized into grid points (Equation 6):

$$g_i \in \mathbb{R}^2 \tag{6}$$

A g_l is connected to g_j via an edge e if and only if there exists a point $x \in \mathbb{R}^d$ that is equally close to g_l and g_j in terms of metric D, as well as closer to g_l and g_j than any other point g_i with

$$\exists\, x \in \mathbb{R}^d : D(x, g_l) = D(x, g_j) \wedge D(x, g_l) < D(x, g_i) \forall i \neq l, j. \tag{7}$$

Equation 7 means that the Delaunay graph (Delaunay, 1934) between the projected points is calculated. Let graph Γ be a pair (V, E) for which the grid points are the vertices $v \in V$, let $\{e_1(l, k)..., e_n(m, j)\} \in E$ be a sequences of edges defining a walk from grid point g_l to g_j, let $d(l, j)$ be the distances between the corresponding high-dimensional data points $\{l, j\}$, then the length $|p_{l,j}| \in P_{l,j}$ is derived from the path

$$p_{l,j} = d(l, k) * e_1, ..., d(m, j) * e_n. \tag{8}$$

Equation 8 means that each edge between two projected points is weighted with the high-dimensional distance between the corresponding high-dimensional data points. Paths always run in a 2D toroidal space, even if the projection was planar and not toroidal. In this 2D toroidal space, the four edges are cyclically connected. Thus, border effects of the projection process can be compensated. Then the shortest path between two grid points g_l, g_j in (Γ, P) is defined by $\tilde{d}(g_l, g_j) = \min\{P_{l,j}\}$. This shortest path between every pair of points can be computed using the Dijkstra algorithm (Dijkstra, 1959). The shortest paths are then used in the clustering process, which involves two choices depending on the structure type in the high-dimensional data (Thrun and Ultsch, 2021b).

Third, let $C_r \subset I$ and $C_q \subset I$ be two partitions with $r, q \in \{1, \ldots, k\}$ and $C_r \cap C_q = \{\}$ for $r \neq q$ and let data points in the partitions be defined by $l \in C_q$ and $j \in C_r$, with powers $k = |C_q|$ and $p = |C_r|$; further, let $\{g_l, g_j\}$ be the nearest neighbors of two partitions $C_r \subset I$ and $C_q \subset I$, then in each case two partitions $\{C_r, C_q\}$ are aggregated bottom-up with either the minimum dispersion of $\{C_r, C_q\}$:

$$\text{connected structures: } S(C_r, C_q) = \sum_{i=1,j=1,i\neq j}^{k,p} \left[k * pk + p * \tilde{d}(g_l, g_j) \right] \tag{9}$$

or with the smallest distance between $\{C_r, C_q\}$:

$$\text{compact structures: } S(C_r, C_q) = \min_{l \in C_r, j \in C_q} \left[\tilde{d}(g_l, g_j) \right]. \tag{10}$$

For each data case (row in the dataset), two partitions $\{c_r, c_q\}$ are aggregated bottom-up with either the least distance (called compact) or the minimum common "spread" (called connected). The algorithm stops when the established number of partitions is reached. This Boolean choice of structure type (either Equation 9 or Equation 10) and the number of partitions can be decided by looking at a specifically defined visualization of high-dimensional structures (Thrun and Ultsch, 2020a), which is the reason why projection methods are used and manifold learning methods are not used. In a benchmarking of thirty-four comparable clustering methods, PBC was the only algorithm that was always able to find the high-dimensional distance or density-based structure of a large diversity of data challenges (Thrun and Ultsch, 2020b).

The specifically defined visualization of high-dimensional structures is called a topographic map with hypsometric tints (Thrun et al., 2016). Hypsometric tints are surface colors that represent ranges of elevation. Here, contour lines are combined with a specific color scale. The color scale is chosen to display various valleys, ridges, and basins: blue colors indicate small distances (sea level), green and brown colors indicate middle distances (low hills), and shades of white colors indicate vast distances (high mountains covered with snow and ice). In this 3D landscape, valleys and basins represent clusters, and the watersheds of hills and mountain ranges represent the borders between clusters. A central problem in clustering – the correct estimation of the number of clusters – is addressed by the topographic map, which assesses the number of clusters (Thrun et al., 2016). Nevertheless, the question remains as to which nonlinear projection method should be chosen.

Usually, the answer depends on the preference of the users and their experience in setting the parameters of the projection method. In this case, we choose Pswarm (Thrun and Ultsch, 2021a, 2021b), the projection method of the DBS that does not require setting any parameters and enables the user to select a specific distance measure. Pswarm involves a swarm of intelligent agents called DataBots (Ultsch, 2000) and is a focusing projection method based on a polar swarm that exploits the concepts of self-organization and swarm intelligence (Thrun and Ultsch, 2021a). During the construction of this type of projection, which is called the learning phase and requires an annealing scheme, structure analysis shifts from global optimization to local distance preservation (focusing). Intelligent agents of Pswarm operate on a toroid grid where positions are coded into polar coordinates, allowing for a precise definition of their movement, neighborhood function, and annealing scheme.

The size of the grid and, in contrast to other focusing projection methods (e.g., Demartines and Hérault, 1995; van der Maaten and Hinton, 2008; Ultsch and Lötsch, 2017), the annealing scheme are data-driven, and, therefore, this method does not require any parameters. During learning, each DataBot moves across the grid or stays in its current position in the search for the most potent scent, meaning that it searches for other agents carrying data with the most similar features to itself with a data-driven decreasing search radius (Thrun and Ultsch, 2021a). The movement of every DataBot is modeled using a game theory approach, and the radius decreases only if a Nash equilibrium is found (Nash, 1951). Contrary to other projection methods and similar to the emergent self-organizing map, a Pswarm projection does not possess a global objective function, allowing the method to apply self-organization and swarm intelligence (Thrun and Ultsch, 2021a).

Obviously, and as mentioned earlier, data must be preprocessed before they can be used in any CA. Typical steps are standardization of the data, decorrelation, selection of a suitable distance measure (Thrun, 2021b), and checking whether high-dimensional structures exist in the data (Thrun, 2020). For simplicity, we use a dataset with known cluster structures, Euclidean distances, and ad hoc standardization methods available through the mirrored-density plot (MD plot) (Thrun et al., 2020a). The MD plot is a schematic plot that is able to detect and visualize the basic properties of empirical distributions that are interesting for data mining tasks, outperforming other typical schematic plots such as the box-whisker diagram or box plot (Tukey, 1977), the violin plot (Hintze and Nelson, 1998), the bean plot (Kampstra, 2008), and the ridgeline plot (Wilke, 2019). The MD plot uses a special case of uniform kernel estimates, which is a density estimation using the number of points within a hypersphere of a fixed radius around each given data point. In this case, the number of points within a hypersphere of each data point is used for the density estimation at the center of the hypersphere.

In Pareto density estimation (PDE), the radius for the hypersphere density estimation is chosen optimally [with respect to] information-theoretic ideas (Ultsch, 2005). Information optimization calls for a radius that enables the hyperspheres to contain maximum information using minimal volume. If a hypersphere has approximately 20 percent of the data on average, it is the source of more than 80 percent of the possible information that any subset of the data can have (Ultsch, 2005). Thus, PDE is particularly suitable for the discovery of structures in continuous data and allows for the discovery of mixtures of Gaussians (Ultsch et al., 2015). In sum, the MD plot is based on mirroring the PDF in a visualization combined with the PDE approach to density estimation. Moreover, it integrates statistical testing, subsampling, and ordering of variables based on statistical criteria and simple standardization approaches within its framework. Furthermore, the MD plot decides if the PDF is estimated or if Dirac delta distributions are visualized because the variable does not have enough unique values to estimate it.

4.4 Steps of Projection-Based Clustering

To apply the DBS method, a few steps must be taken. The initial part of the procedure consists of performing a distribution analysis, a standardization, and a decorrelation of the data. Afterwards, the three steps of the PBC are applied. Finally, a very short excursion into visual analytics is made. Unlike the other sections, the generalized scripts for the R environment (R Development Core Team, 2011) related to this part of the analysis will also be supplied in this section. The R code related to specific applications and case studies, will be provided in *Machine Learning for Archaeological Applications in R*. The R libraries that are used are:

```
library(DatabionicSwarm)
library(GeneralizedUmatrix)
library(ProjectionBasedClustering)
```

4.4.1 Preprocessing

First, the data are read in the "cellWise" package, and missing values (if any) must be accounted for:

```
library(cellWise)
data(data_glass)
Data=as.matrix(data_glass)
dim(Data)
## [1] 180 750
```

We look into the distributions using MD plots (Thrun et al., 2020a) with the next script:

```
library(DataVisualizations)
MDplot(Data,RobustGaussian = F,Ordering = "Columnwise")
# MD plot of all variables
```

Significant differences in the variance of distributions are observable in Figure 13. In this figure, we can see that some variables at the left edge of the spectra have no information. If we zoom in on this region by plotting only the first thirty columns, as shown in Figure 14, we can see that several columns do not hold any information:

```
MDplot(Data[,1:30],RobustGaussian = F,Ordering =
"Columnwise")
#MD plot of columns 1 to 30
```

Because of the non-Gaussianity (e.g., V16) and the multimodality (e.g., V23) of the features, the well-known *z*-transformation is not advisable. Therefore, columns 1 to 14 were deleted as follows:

```
Data=Data[,-c(1:14)]
```

There are too many features to account for each distribution of each feature separately. Hence, we select a robust transformation to consider variances:

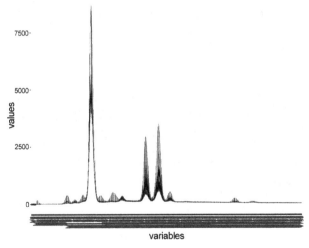

Figure 13 An MD plot of all variables.

Note: Colour version available at www.cambridge.org/knowledge_materials.

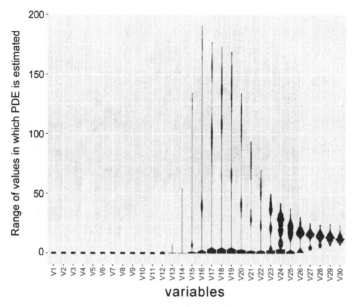

Figure 14 An MD plot (Thrun et al., 2020a) of the first thirty variables where the estimated PDF for each variable is presented as a blue violin; the estimation is performed with the parameter-free PDE (Ultsch, 2005). As can be seen, the first thirteen variables contain no information.

Note: Colour version available at www.cambridge.org/knowledge_materials.

```
Transformed=RobustNormalization(Data,Capped = T)
MDplot(Transformed,RobustGaussian = F,Ordering = "Columnwise")
```

The result is shown in Figure 15. Finally, the features are normalized between zero and one, taking advantage of the "Euclidean distances" properties. Usually, more advanced standardization procedures should be applied.

Correlations can be verified with a Pixelmatrix, as shown in Figure 16:

```
cors=cor(Transformed,method = "spearman")
cors[upper.tri(cors,diag = T)]=0
Pixelmatrix(cors)
```

In this figure, strong linear correlations are indicated by red or blue tones (medium gray and dark gray, respectively, in a grayscale image), while no correlation is shown in yellow (light gray in a grayscale image). Correlations must be accounted for because, otherwise, the weights in the distance matrix are not equal per feature:

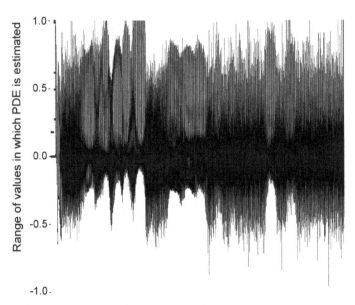

Figure 15 An MD plot showing the straightforward selection and normalization of features.

Note: Colour version available at www.cambridge.org/knowledge_materials.

```
ind=which(abs(Transformed)>0.8,arr.ind = T)
colstodelete=unique(ind[,1])
DecorrelatedTransformed=Transformed[,-colstodelete]
```

Next, Pswarm either accepts a data matrix and automatically computes the Euclidean distances or requires a specific distance matrix of the choice of the user:

```
# Preparing the data for the first module (Projection of high-
dimensional data to low
#dimensions using pswarm)
library(parallelDist)
InputDistances=as.matrix
(parallelDist(DecorrelatedTransformed))
```

4.4.2 First Step: Generate Projection Using Pswarm

In this step, a nonlinear DR approach is used by exploiting the concepts of swarm intelligence, self-organization, and emergence (Thrun and Ultsch, 2021a). High-dimensional data are projected into a 2D space by the Pswarm using intelligent agents operating on a toroidal and polar grid:

```
projection=Pswarm(InputDistances)
```

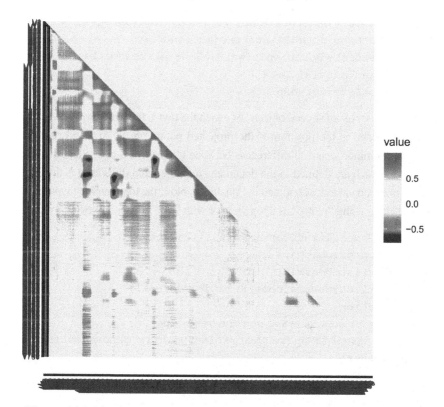

Figure 16 A Pixelmatrix indicating strong linear correlations in red or blue (medium gray and dark gray, respectively, in a grayscale image) and no correlation in yellow (light gray in a grayscale image). By setting the upper triangle of the correlation matrix to zero in the code, we can ignore here the yellow color of the upper triangle of the Pixelmatrix.

Note: Colour version available at www.cambridge.org/knowledge_materials.

4.4.3 Second Step: Simultaneously Quantize Projection Points and Generate a Topographic Map

The function "GeneratePswarmVisualization" creates all required objects to plot the topographic map. The specific algorithm behind this function is published in Thrun (2018) and requires a given number of lines L and columns C as a tertiary input that defines the size of the 2D plane and is stored in the vector LC. For other projection methods, the more generalized function "GeneralizedUmatrix:: GeneralizedUmatrix()" is preferable; this function was published in Thrun and Ultsch (2020b) and differs from the first function in certain characteristics (e.g., LC is estimated internally). Both approaches require the projected points and the dataset. The generalized U-matrix algorithm is defined in Thrun and Ultsch (2020b):

```
genUmatrxList= GeneratePswarmVisualization(Data,
projection$ProjectedPoints,projection$LC)
#genUmatrxList= DatabionicSwarm::GeneralizedUmatrix::
GeneralizedUmatrix((Data,
projection$ProjectedPoints)
```

The output is a list of several objects, of which the first is the generalized U-matrix and the second is the position of the projected points on the 3D landscape. In addition to minor technical differences between the projected points and the best matches, which are defined in the documentation, the main difference is that best matches are quantized, as outlined in Equation 6. Now, the topographic map can be shown either using "plotly" as a top view or with "rgl" in interactive 3D:

```
library(GeneralizedUmatrix)visualization <-
TopviewTopographicMap(
genUmatrxList$Umatrix,
genUmatrxList$Bestmatches,ExtendBorders=10)
visualization
## For the 3D view, please use the next code
# plotTopographicMap(genUmatrxList$Umatrix,genUmatrxList
$Bestmatches)
```

Figure 17 shows an example of a top-view toroidal topographic map. "Toroidal" means that all borders are cyclically connected. Each data row is visualized as a projected point. To vividly show the toroidal structure, the borders of the topographic map are extended. One could visualize each point four times in a tiled display (Lötsch et al., 2018), but it is more straightforward to visualize them only once. Mountains and valleys display high-dimensional distance-based structures. Density-based structures are accounted through use of the Pswarm projection method (Thrun and Ultsch, 2021a). Using another projection method, one could also investigate density-based structures with the U-Matrix (Ultsch, 2003).

The interpretation of the map is clearer in a color display than in grayscale; in this, every point colored in magenta is shown only once in this four-tiles presentation. The tiled display repeats the visualization of the structures in order to account for border effects.

4.4.4 Third Step: Cluster Analysis

The clustering is performed with the code below:

```
Cls=DBSclustering(k=4, Data,
genUmatrxList$Bestmatches, genUmatrxList$LC,StructureType =
F, PlotIt=T)
```

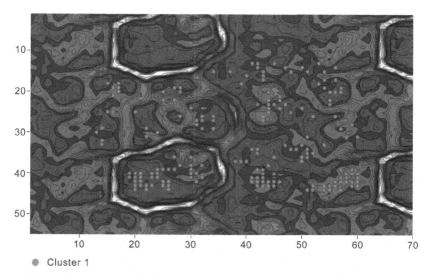

● Cluster 1

Figure 17 An example of a top-view toroidal topographic map showing three valleys and one volcano in which an outlier lies, resulting in the assumption of four clusters.

Note: Colour version available at www.cambridge.org/knowledge_materials.

The number of clusters (k) is derived from the number of valleys visible in the topographic map (volcanos are counted as separate clusters in Figure 17, so $k = 4$). The next three parameters are the data, the position of the projected points, and the size of the 2D plane. The Boolean parameter is called StructureType (see Equations 9 and 10). A dendrogram can be additionally plotted with "PlotIt"; this is shown in Figure 18 (which agrees with the topographic map of Figure 17). The quantized projected points are stored for historical reasons in a variable called "Bestmatches," indicating a closed connection of the topographic map to the well-known U-matrix (Ultsch and Siemon, 1990) and the emergent self-organizing map (Ultsch, 1999). "Cls" is the numerical vector storing 1 to k number of the length of the number of rows of data defining the clustering. If other projection methods are preferred, one can also use the integrated approach of the FCPS package for R; for example, with "NerV" (Venna et al., 2010):

```
FCPS::AutomaticProjectionBasedClustering(DataOrDistances
= Data,ClusterNo = 4,StructureType = F,PlotMap
= T,Type = "NerV")
```

Clustering is verified by inspecting the topographic map of Figure 19 (Thrun et al., 2016):

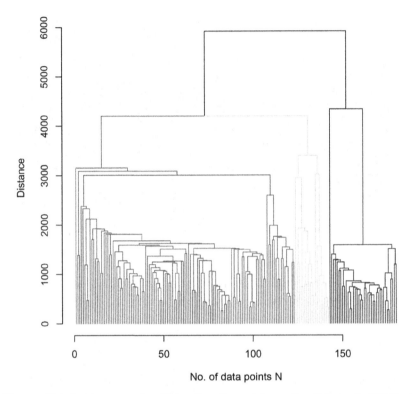

Figure 18 A dendrogram visualizing the ultrametric portion (Murtagh, 2004) of the used distance measure. Large steps in the dendrogram indicate a good cut; in this figure, it is cut into four clusters.

Note: Colour version available at www.cambridge.org/knowledge_materials.

```
# Top view of clusters Clusters <- TopviewTopographicMap(
genUmatrxList$Umatrix,
genUmatrxList$Bestmatches,
Cls,ExtendBorders=10)
Clusters
# For the 3D plot, use the next code
# plotTopographicMap(genUmatrxList$Umatrix,genUmatrxList
$Bestmatches,Cls)
```

If the clustering does not overlap entirely with the 3D landscape, the user can improve it interactively; for this step, see Thrun et al. (2020b):

```
#Cls=interactiveClustering(genUmatrxList$Umatrix,
genUmatrxList$Bestmatches,Cls = Cls)
#imx=interactiveGeneralizedUmatrixIsland(genUmatrxList
```

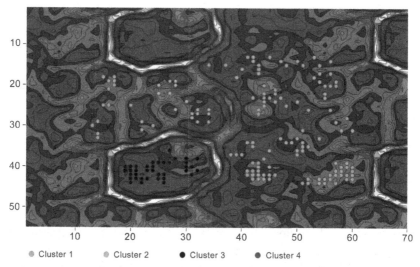

● Cluster 1   ● Cluster 2   ● Cluster 3   ● Cluster 4

Figure 19 Clustering corresponds well with the topographic map.
The map should be in a color display to be understandable. The main cluster is
depicted by points colored in magenta (light gray in a grayscale image), clearly
divided from the two minor clusters consisting of yellow and black points
(white and black, respectively, in a grayscale image). The outlier
lies in its own volcano.

Note: Colour version available at www.cambridge.org/knowledge_materials.

```
$Umatrix,genUmatrxList$Bestmatches,Cls = Cls)
# plotTopographicMap(genUmatrxList$Umatrix,genUmatrxList
$Bestmatches,Cls,imx)
```

For a published example, see López-García et al. (2020), in which additionally
the function "interactiveGeneralizedUmatrixIsland" was interactively used to
cut out a nontoroidal island from the toroidal visualization. The topographic
map can also be displayed in 3D to be presented to domain experts (Thrun et al.,
2016). For the technical steps to achieve a 3D print, please read the documentation. Note that Pswarm is a stochastic projection method (see Thrun [2018] for
details), meaning that the results of the visualization and clustering can vary
depending on the trial. To ensure that the procedure yields a stable solution, it is
suggested to apply the three steps more than once.

4.4.5 Fourth Step: Validation of the Model

In any scientific research, it is important to validate the obtained results by
means of a statistical procedure. This allows evaluation of whether the results
can be considered adequate enough to provide accurate predictions and if the

conclusions are valid enough to support the inference process by identifying the relationships that are significant. Thus, it is necessary to include a procedure to assess the outcome of the clustering in a quantitative and objective manner (Jain and Dubes, 1988). The clustering validation method provides a quality measure or model validation index according to certain criteria; it is used to establish if the model fits the data well or if it represents only a spurious solution. To calculate the quantitative measure of accuracy, a supervised index can be used, defined by Equation 11:

$$\text{Accuracy } [\%] = \frac{\text{No. of true positives}}{\text{No. of cases}} \tag{11}$$

where the number of true positives is the number of labeled data points for which the label defined by a first classification is identical to the label defined for a second classification in supervised machine learning. However, in unsupervised machine learning, the clustering labels are arbitrary defined, which makes a direct application impossible. Hence, the best permutation of all the clustering labels – that is, the one with the highest accuracy – should be selected (Thrun, 2018). The closer the value is to 100%, the better the adjustment of the model.

In addition to this index, there are two other nonsupervised indices used to externally evaluate the quality of the clustering obtained with the algorithms: the silhouette plot (Kaufman and Rousseeuw, 2005) and the heatmap (Wilkinson and Friendly, 2009). The silhouette plot (see example in Figure 20) is a graphic representation of the ideal number of clusters; each group is represented by a silhouette within a range of values from −1 to +1. The silhouette width is a metric for assessing how similar an object is to its own group (cohesion) compared to other groups (separation). A value close to +1 indicates that the samples are correctly allocated and that they are far from the neighboring groups. A value of 0 would indicate that some of the observations are very close to the decision limit between two neighboring clusters (i.e., overlapping groups), and negative values indicate that the samples might have been assigned to the wrong cluster. If the average silhouette value is > 0.5, the clustering is considered reasonable; an average value < 0.2 should be interpreted as a lack of substantial clustering structure. One has to use the silhouette plot with great caution since it accounts only for spherical cluster structures in data and penalizes heavily nonspherical cluster structures (Thrun, 2021a).

The generic R code for displaying the silhouette plot is:

```
library(DataVisualizations)
Silhouetteplot(Data, Cls = Cls)
```

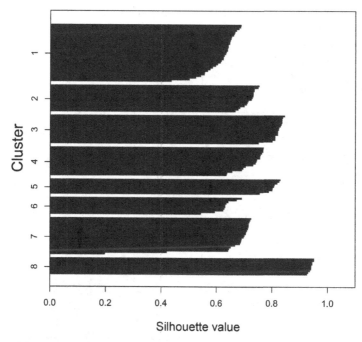

Figure 20 An example of a silhouette plot clearly marking the presence of eight clusters, with no negative or zero value observations.

Note: Colour version available at www.cambridge.org/knowledge_materials.

On the other hand, the heatmap (see example in Figure 21) is a graphical representation of high-dimensional data that shows how similar the objects are within a cluster and dissimilar outside of it. A heatmap projects in a rectangular grid the distances of the clusters ordered by variations in color, revealing the hierarchical cluster structure in a data matrix (Wilkinson and Friendly, 2009). The results of a clustering are displayed in the form of a color-shaded matrix, which places variables in rows and columns and colors the cells (pixels) within the table or spreadsheet according to their values in the data matrix. Darker colors (from dark blue to teal) indicate small intracluster distances; medium distances are displayed in yellow shades; and large inter-cluster distances are shown in orange and red colors. The clusters are divided by black lines. The clustering will be considered valid if the intracluster distances are distinctively smaller than the intercluster distances in the heatmap (Thrun, 2018). One has to use the heatmap with caution because the underlying assumption is that distance-based structures are prevalent in the data. Consequently, density-based structures are penalized heavily. To generate a heatmap in R, the following code is used:

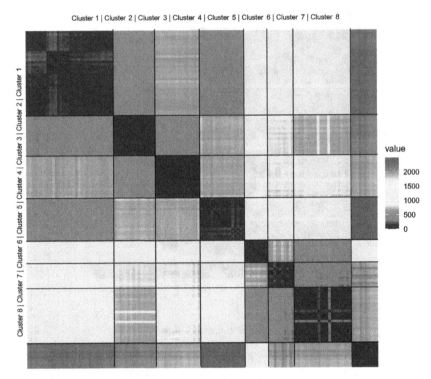

Cluster 1 | Cluster 2 | Cluster 3 | Cluster 4 | Cluster 5 | Cluster 6 | Cluster 7 | Cluster 8

Figure 21 An example of a heatmap showing the existence of eight groups in a dataset (dark blue or dark gray squares along the central diagonal).

Note: Colour version available at www.cambridge.org/knowledge_materials.

```
library(DataVisualizations)
Heatmap(as.matrix(dist(Data)), Cls = Cls)
```

One last way to evaluate the result of a clustering is by a contingency table, in which the groups are accommodated in the rows and are the result of the clustering in the columns. In a good classification scheme, the main values will be located in the central diagonal, and the row and column percentages will sum to 100%. This contingency table is computed by the following R code:

```
rm(list=ls())library(FCPS)
DataRaw <-
read.csv(&quot;C:\\Hans\\Mayas_H\\IXT_38_865\\cinco_gps\
\IXTEP5Emsc_SG\\Dos_interv_sin119 c
on_Cls.csv";, header = T)
str(DataRaw)
Cls_prior=DataRaw$Cls
```

```
Cls_prior
ind=which(colnames(DataRaw)!=";Cls&quot")
Data=as.matrix(DataRaw[,ind])
ContingencyTableSummary=function(RowCls, ColCls)
{
# contingency table of two Cls
# INPUT
# RowCls,bCls vector of class identifiers (i.e. integers or
NaN's) of the same length
# OUTPUT list with these elements:
# cTab cTab(i,j) contains the count of all Instances where the
i-th class in RowCls
#equals the j-th class inColCls
# rowID the different classes in RowCls, corresponding to the
rows of cTab
# colID the different classes inColCls, corresponding to the
columns of cTab
# RowClassCount, RowClassPercentages instance count and per-
centages of classes in
#RowCls sorted according rowID
# ColClassCount, ColClassPercentages instance count and per-
centages of classes #inColCls
#sorted according colID
RowID = length(unique(RowCls))
ColID = length(unique(ColCls))
Ctable = table(RowCls, ColCls)
AllinTab = sum(Ctable)
ColumnSum = colSums(Ctable)
ColPercentage = round(ColumnSum/AllinTab * 100, 2)
RowSum = rowSums(Ctable)
RowPercentage = round(RowSum/AllinTab * 100, 2)
Rows <- rbind(round(Ctable), ColumnSum, ColPercentage)
Xtable <- cbind(Rows, c(RowSum, AllinTab, 0), c(RowPercentage,
0, 100))
colnames(Xtable) = c(1:ColID, "RowSum", "RowPercentage")
return(Xtable)
}
Table=ContingencyTableSummary(Cls_prior)
Table
```

It is not necessary to use all four validation indices, but at least two should be considered for robustly and objectively assessing whether the procedure is correct and the model fits the data.

5 Final Comments

The conventional methods applied in archaeological and archaeometric research for clustering/classifying cultural materials present several limitations since they consider that the extraction of patterns in the data can be performed routinely without going too deep into the requirements of the models and the behavior of the data. In the different sections of this Element, we provided a list of factors that should be considered when the objective is to reconstruct behavior patterns related to ancient human groups, such as the use of raw material deposits, long-distance trade, or different manufacturing techniques. Whatever case is being investigated, it is recommended to pay close attention to the collection of information and the intrinsic nature of the data you are dealing with, as well as to use the more robust versions of the methods.

Classical multivariate methods present severe problems caused by the structures they find in the data, theoretical assumptions that cannot be fulfilled, and an absence of tools for data diagnosis, outlier detection, and model validation, factors that are fundamental in data analysis. The statistical methods described in this Element offer a more robust way to process quantitative archaeological data in both low-dimensional (such as compositional data) and high-dimensional (spectral data) spaces. These methods are centered on model-based clustering, through variable selection with iPLS and PBC.

The methods proposed in the sections represent an efficient and objective way to discriminate between different groups of data (e.g., natural raw material deposits and subsources) regardless of the sample size or the number of variables, which are part of the weaknesses of classical multivariate methods. For example, the PBC method provides a parameter-free high-dimensional data visualization technique obtained with the algorithm known as U-matrix (Ultsch and Siemon, 1990). These methods are proven to perform well in the search for structures in data, without incurring errors such as overlapping or misassignment of samples to groups.

There are multivariate methods for each type of variable or their combinations and relationships. These can yield much information, like the structure and the interrelation present in the data and the quality of the research. Currently, we have very advanced algorithms that allow the translation of many meaningless data into groups with differentiable natural structures. As archaeologists, we do not have to learn by heart all the formulas and mathematical procedures of the techniques, but it is always good that we know what the method consists of, what kind of data it is used for, and how we can interpret the results accurately, always keeping in mind the theoretical assumptions of the techniques and their limitations. We understand that the development of new data processing methods and algorithms is advancing rapidly today. That is why we urge the reader to stay updated and always in search of new scientific approaches that allow for solving old problems in new ways.

Abbreviations

alr	additive log-ratio
BIC	Bayesian information criterion
CA	cluster analysis
CAIS	Center for Applied Isotope Studies
CEM	classification expectation maximization
clr	centered log-ratio
CluPA	hierarchical cluster-based peak alignment
CRMs	certified reference materials
DA	discriminant analysis
DBS	databionic swarm
DR	dimensionality reduction
EM	expectation maximization
EMSC	extended multiplicative signal correction
FAST-MCD	fast minimum covariance determinant
FCPS	Fundamental Clustering Problems Suite
FT-IR	Fourier transform infrared spectroscopy
ICP–MS	inductively coupled plasma–mass spectrometry
ICL	integrated complete likelihood
ilr	isometric log-ratio
iPLS	interval partial least squares
KNN	K-nearest neighbors (also known as K-NN)
LDA	linear discriminant analysis
LVs	latent variables
MAP	maximum a posteriori probability
MCD	minimum covariance determinant
MD plot	mirrored-density plot
ML	maximization of log-likelihood
NN	nearest neighbors

NAA	neutron activation analysis
NEC	normalized entropy criterion
NPE	neighborhood proportion error
ODi	orthogonal distance
PBC	projection-based clustering
PCA	principal component analysis
PCs	principal components
PDE	Pareto density estimation
PDF	probability density function
PLS	partial least squares
PP	projection pursuit
pXRF	portable X-ray fluorescence
QDA	quadratic discriminant analysis
RMSECV	root mean squared error of cross-validation
RMSEP	root mean squared error of prediction
ROBPCA	robust principal component analysis
SBP	sequential binary partition
SDi	score distance
SEM	stochastic expectation maximization
SG	Savitzky–Golay filter
SNE	stochastic neighbor embedding
SSC	semisupervised classification
SS	semisupervised
SVD	singular values decomposition
VBDL	values below detection limits
XRF	X-ray fluorescence

References

Ackerman, M. (2012). Towards theoretical foundations of clustering. PhD thesis, David R. Cheriton School of Computer Science, University of Waterloo, ON.

Adolfsson, A., Ackerman, M. & Brownstein, N. C. (2019). To cluster, or not to cluster: An analysis of clusterability methods. *Pattern Recognition*, **88**, 13–26.

Afseth, N. K. & Kohler, A. (2012). Extended multiplicative signal correction in vibrational spectroscopy, a tutorial. *Chemometrics and Intelligent Laboratory Systems*, **117**, 92–99.

Aitchison, J. (1986). *The Statistical Analysis of Compositional Data*. London: Chapman & Hall.

Aitchison, J., Barceló-Vidal, C. & Pawlowsky-Glahn, V. (2002). Some comments on compositional data analysis in archaeometry, in particular the fallacies in Tangri and Wright's dismissal of log ratio analysis. *Archaeometry*, **44**(2), 295–304.

Alelyani, S., Tang, J. & Liu, H. (2014). Feature selection for clustering: A review. In C. C. Aggarwal and C. K. Reddy, eds., *Data Clustering: Algorithms and Applications*, Vol. 29. Hoboken, NJ: CRC Press, pp. 1–33.

Alqurashi, T. & Wang, W. (2019). Clustering ensemble method. *International Journal of Machine Learning and Cybernetics*, **10**(6), 1227–1246.

Ball, F. & Geyer-Schulz, A. (2018). Invariant graph partition comparison measures. *Symmetry*, **10**(10), 1–27.

Barca, D., Crisci, G. M. & Miriello, D. (2019). Chapter 11 Obsidian and volcanic glass shards: Characterization and provenancing. In G. Artioli and R. Oberti, eds., *The Contribution of Mineralogy to Cultural Heritage*, Vol. 20 of EMU Notes in Mineralogy. London: European Mineralogical Union and the Mineralogical Society of Great Britain & Ireland, pp. 393–409.

Barwick, V. (2003). *Preparation of Calibration Curves: A Guide to Best Practice*. Technical report no. LGC/VAM/2003/032. https://biosearch-cdn .azureedge.net/assetsv6/Calibration-curve-guide.pdf.

Baudry, J. P., Raftery, A. E., Celeux, G., Lo, K. & Gottardo, R. (2010). Combining mixture components for clustering. *Journal of Computational and Graphical Statistics*, **9**(2), 332–353.

Baxter, M. J. (1995). Standardization and transformation in principal component analysis, with applications to archaeometry. *Journal of the Royal Statistical Society: Series C (Applied Statistics)*, **44**(4), 513–527.

Baxter, M. J. (2003). *Statistics in Archaeology*. Oxford: Oxford University Press.

Baxter, M. J. (2015). *Notes on Quantitative Archaeology and R*. www.mike metrics.com/download/mark_dl/Book (accessed November 1, 2019).

Baxter, M. J. & Buck, C. (2000). Data handling and statistical analysis. In E. Ciliberto and G. Spoto, eds., *Modern Analytical Methods in Art and Archaeology*. New York: Wiley-Interscience, pp. 681–746.

Beirnaert, C., Meysman, P., Vu, T. N., Hermans, N., Apers, S., Pieters, L., Covaci, A. & Laukens, K. (2018). Speaq 2.0: A complete workflow for high-throughput 1D NMR spectra processing and quantification. *PLoS Computational Biology*, **14**(3), e1006018.

Bellman, R. E. (1961). *Adaptive Control Processes: A Guided Tour*. Princeton, NJ: Princeton University Press.

Benaglia, T., Chauveau, D., Hunter, D. R. & Young, D. (2009). Mixtools: An R package for analyzing finite mixture models. *Journal of Statistical Software*, **32**(6), 1–29.

Ben-Hur, A. & Guyon, I. (2003). Detecting stable clusters using principal component analysis. In M. J. Brownstein and A. Kohodursky, eds., *Functional Genomics: Methods and Protocols*. Geneva: Humana Press, pp. 159–182.

Biecek, P., Szczurek, E., Vingron, M. & Tiuryn, J. (2012). The R package bgmm: Mixture modeling with uncertain knowledge. *Journal of Statistical Software*, **47**(3), 1–32.

Biernacki, C., Celeux, G. & Govaert, G. (2000). Assessing a mixture model for clustering with the integrated completed likelihood. *IEEE Transactions on Pattern Analysis and Machine Intelligence*, **22**(7), 719–725.

Biernacki, C., Celeux, G., Govaert, G. & Langrognet, F. (2006). Model-based cluster and discriminant analysis with the Mixmod software. *Computational Statistics and Data Analysis*, **51**(2), 587–600.

Biernacki, C., Marbac, M. & Vandewalle, V. (2019). *Package "ClusVis": [A] Gaussian-based Visualization of Gaussian and Non-Gaussian Model-Based Clustering*. https://cran.r-project.org/web/packages/ClusVis/ClusVis.pdf (accessed August 18, 2019).

Biernacki, C., Marbac, M. & Vandewalle, V. (2021). Gaussian-based visualization of Gaussian and non-Gaussian-based clustering. *Journal of Classification*, **38**, 129–157.

Bishop, R. L. & Neff, H. (1989). Compositional data analysis in archaeology. In R. O. Allen, ed., *Archaeological Chemistry IV*. Advances in Chemistry Series 220. Washington, DC: American Chemical Society, pp. 576–586.

Bolin, J. H., Edwards, J. M., Holmes, W. H. & Cassady, J. C. (2014). Applications of cluster analysis to the creation of perfectionism profiles: A comparison of two clustering approaches. *Frontiers in Psychology*, **5**, article 343. https://doi.org/10.3389/fpsyg.2014.00343.

Bonner, R. E. (1964). On some clustering technique. *IBM Journal of Research and Development*, **8**(1), 22–32.

Bouveyron, C. & Brunet-Saumard, C. (2014). Model-based clustering of high-dimensional data: A review. *Computational Statistics and Data Analysis*, **71**, 52–78.

Bouveyron, C., Hammer, B. & Villmann, T. (2012). Recent developments in clustering algorithms. In M. Verleysen, ed., *Proceedings of the 20th European Symposium on Artificial Neural Networks*. Bruges, Belgium: Computational Intelligence and Machine Learning, pp. 447–458.

Buck, C. E. & Litton, C. D. (1996). Mixtures, Bayes and archaeology. In J. M. Bernado, J. O. Berger, A. P. Dawid, and A. F. M. Smith, eds., *Bayesian Statistics 5*. Oxford: Clarendon Press, pp. 499–506.

Carter, T., Batist, Z., Campeau, K., Garfinkel, Y. & Streit, K. (2017). Investigating pottery neolithic socio-economic "regression" in the Southern Levant: Characterising obsidian consumption at Sha'ar Hagolan (N. Israel). *Journal of Archaeological Science: Reports*, **15**, 305–317.

Ceccarelli, L., Rossetti, I., Primavesi, L. & Stoddart, S. (2016). Non-destructive method for the identification of ceramic production by portable X-rays fluorescence (pXRF): A case study of amphorae manufacture in central Italy. *Journal of Archaeological Science: Reports*, **10**, 253–262.

Chang, W. C. (1983). On using principal components before separating a mixture of two multivariate normal distributions. *Journal of the Royal Statistical Society: Series C (Applied Statistics)*, **32**(3), 267–275.

Chen, W. & Maitra, R. (2019). *EMCluster: EM Algorithm for Model-Based Clustering of Finite Mixture Gaussian Distribution*. https://CRAN.R-project.org/package=EMCluster (accessed November 15, 2020).

Daszykowski, M., Kaczmarek, K., Stanimirova, I., Vander Heyden, Y. & Walczak, B. (2007). Robust SIMCA-bounding influence of outliers. *Chemometrics and Intelligent Laboratory Systems*, **87**(1), 95–103.

Davies, D. L. & Bouldin, D. W. (1979). A cluster separation measure. *IEEE Transactions on Pattern Analysis and Machine Intelligence*, **PAMI-1**(2), 224–227.

Dean, E. A., Neff, H., Glascock, M. D. & Speakman, R. J. (2007). Sourcing the palygorskite used in Maya blue: A pilot study comparing the results of INAA and LA-ICP-MS. *Latin American Antiquity*, **18**(1), 44–58.

Delaunay, B. (1934). Sur la sphere vide: A la memoire de Georges Voronoi. *Bulletin de l'Académie des Sciences de l'URSS: Classe des sciences mathématiques et naturelles*, **6**, 793–800.

Demartines, P. & Hérault, J. (1995). CCA: "Curvilinear Component Analysis." In *Proceedings of 15°Colloque sur le Traitement du Signal et des Images*,

Vol. 199. Juan-les-pins, France: Groupe d'Etudes du Traitement du Signal et des Images (GRETSI), pp. 921–924.

Descantes, C., Speakman, R. & Glascock, M. (2008). Compositional studies of Caribbean ceramics: An introduction to instrumental neutron activation analysis. *Journal of Caribbean Archaeology, Special Publication No. 2: An Exploratory Study into the Chemical Characterization of Caribbean Ceramics*, 1–14.

Dijkstra, E. W. (1959). A note on two problems in connexion with graphs. *Numerische mathematik*, **1**, 269–271.

Doran, J. & Hodson, F. R. (1975). *Mathematics and Computers in Archaeology*. Cambridge, MA: Harvard University Press.

Dos Santos Panero, P., dos Santos Panero, F., dos Santos Panero, J. & Bezerra da Silva, H. E. (2013). Application of extended multiplicative signal correction to short-wavelength near infrared spectra of moisture in marzipan. *Journal of Data Analysis and Information Processing*, **1**(3), 30–34.

Duda, R. O., Hart, P. E. & Stork, D. G. (2001). *Pattern Classification*, 2nd ed. New York: John Wiley & Sons.

Dunn, J. C. (1974). Well-separated clusters and optimal fuzzy partitions. *Journal of Cybernetics*, **4**(1), 95–104.

Egozcue, J. J. & Pawlowsky-Glahn, V. (2005). Groups of parts and their balances in compositional data analysis. *Mathematical Geology*, **37**(7), 795–828.

Egozcue, J. J. & Pawlowsky-Glahn, V. (2011). Análisis composicional de datos en Ciencias Geoambientales. *Boletín Geológico y Minero*, **122**(4), 439–452.

Egozcue, J. J., Pawlowsky-Glahn, V., Mateu-Figueras, G. & Barceló-Vidal, C. (2003). Isometric logratio transformations for compositional data analysis. *Mathematical Geology*, **35**(3), 279–300.

Egozcue Rubí, J. J., Tolosana-Delgado, R., Jarauta Bragulat, E., Ortego Martínez, M. I. & Díaz Barrero, J. L. (2011). Análisis de datos composicionales: Aguas, contaminantes, recursos, sociología . . . *Jornada de Recerca i Innovació a l'Escola de Camins. Comunicació de congrés presented at the Jornada de Recerca i Innovació a l'Escola de Camins*. Barcelona: Universitat Politècnica de Catalunya, Escola Tècnica Superior d'Enginyers de Camins Canals i Ports de Barcelona.

Elson, C., Nichols, D., Cecil, L. & Glascock, M. C. (2006). *Aztec Elites and the Post Classic Economy: Instrumental Neutron Activation Analysis (INAA) of Museum Collections from Chiconautla, México*. Report submitted to FAMSI. www.famsi.org/reports/03019/index.html (accessed August 20, 2020).

Engelen, S. & Hubert, M. (2004). Fast cross-validation for robust PCA. In J. Antoch, ed., *Proceedings in Computational Statistics COMPSTAT'2004 Symposium*. Heidelberg: Physica/Springer, pp. 989–996.

Estivill-Castro, V. (2002). Why so many clustering algorithms: A position paper. *ACM SIGKDD Explorations Newsletter*, **4**(1), 65–75.

Everitt, B. S. & Hand, D. J. (1981). *Finite Mixture Distributions*. Dordrecht: Springer Netherlands.

Everitt, B. S., Landau, S., Leese, M. & Stahl, D. (2011). *Cluster Analysis*, 5th ed. Vol. 848 of Wiley Series in Probability and Statistics. Chichester, UK: John Wiley & Sons.

Ferguson, J. R. & Glascock, M. D. (2007). *Instrumental Neutron Activation Analysis of Ionian Cups from the Western Mediterranean*. Technical report prepared for Ulrike Krotscheck of the Department of Classics, Standford CA. http://blogs.evergreen.edu/ulrikek/files/2016/10/krotscheck-2007-report.pdf (accessed July 15, 2020).

Filzmoser, P. & Todorov, V. (2011). Review of robust multivariate statistical methods in high dimension. *Analytica Chimica Acta*, **705**(1–2), 2–14.

Filzmoser, P., Gussenbauer, J. & Templ, M. (2016). *Detecting Outliers in Household Consumption Survey Data*. Vienna University of Technology Technical Report. www.ihsn.org/node/695 (accessed May 9, 2022).

Filzmoser, P., Hron, K. & Reimann, C. (2009). Principal component analysis for compositional data with outliers. *Environmetrics*, **20**, 621–632.

Fop, M. & Murphy, T. B. (2018). Variable selection methods for model-based clustering. *Statistics Surveys*, **12**, 1–48.

Fraley, C. & Raftery, A. E. (1998). How many clusters? Which clustering method? Answers via model-based cluster analysis. *Computer Journal*, **41**(8), 578–588.

Fraley, C. & Raftery, A. E. (2002). Model-based clustering, discriminant analysis and density estimation. *Journal of the American Statistical Association*, **97**(458), 611–631.

Fraley, C., Raftery, A. E., Murphy, T. B. & Scrucca, L. (2012). *mclust Version 4 for R: Normal Mixture Modeling for Model-Based Clustering, Classification, and Density Estimation*. Technical report no. 597. Department of Statistics, University of Washington. https://stat.uw.edu/sites/default/files/files/reports/2012/tr597.pdf (accessed April 14, 2024).

Gallhofer, D. & Lottermoser, B. G. (2018). The influence of spectral interferences on critical element determination with portable X-ray fluorescence (pXRF). *Minerals*, **8**(8), 320.

George, E. I. & McCulloch, R. E. (1993). Variable selection via Gibbs sampling. *Journal of the American Statistical Association*, **88**(423), 881–889.

George, E. I. & McCulloch, R. E. (1997). Approaches for Bayesian variable selection. *Statistica Sinica*, **7**, 339–373.

Glascock, M. D. (1992). Characterization of archaeological ceramics at MURR by neutron activation analysis and multivariate statistics. In H. Neff, ed., *Chemical Characterization of Ceramic Pastes in Archaeology*. Vol. 7 of Monographs in World Archaeology. Madison, WI: Prehistory Press, pp. 11–26.

Glascock, M. D. (1994). New World obsidian: Recent investigations. In D. A. Scott and P. Meyers, eds., *Archaeometry of Pre-Columbian Sites and Artifacts: Proceedings of a Symposium*. Los Angeles, CA: UCLA Institute of Archaeology and Getty Conservation Institute, pp. 113–134.

Glascock, M. D. (2011). Chapter 8 Comparison and contrast between XRF and NAA: Used for characterization of obsidian sources in Central Mexico. In M. S. Shackley, ed., *X-ray Fluorescence Spectrometry (XRF) in Geoarchaeology*. New York: Springer, pp. 161–192.

Glascock, M. D. & Ferguson, J. R. (2012). *Report on the Analysis of Obsidian Source Samples by Multiple Analytical Methods*. Report for Bruce Kaiser on XRF01-40. Archaeometry Laboratory, University of Missouri. www.researchgate.net/publication/236850163_Report_on_the_Analysis_of_Obsidian_Source_Samples_by_Multiple_Analytical_Methods.

Glascock, M. D. & Neff, H. (2003). Neutron activation analysis and provenance research in archaeology. *Measurement Science and Technology*, **14**(9), 1516–1526.

Glascock, M. D., Braswell, G. E. & Cobean, R. H. (1998). A systematic approach to obsidian source characterization. In M. S. Shackley, ed., *Archaeological Obsidian Studies*. Vol 3 of Advances in Archaeological and Museum Science. Boston, MA: Springer, pp. 15–65.

Glascock, M. D., Elam, J. & Cobean, R. H. (1988). Differentiation of obsidian sources in Mesoamerica. In R. M. Farquahr, R. G. V. Hancock, and L. A. Pavlish, eds., *Proceedings of the 26th International Symposium on Archaeometry*. Toronto: Archaeometry Laboratory, University of Toronto, pp. 245–251.

Grün, B. (2019). Chapter 8 Model-based clustering. In S. Frühwirth-Schnatter, G. Celeux, and C. P. Robert, eds., *Handbook of Mixture Analysis*. Boca Raton, FL: CRC Press, pp. 1–36.

Handl, J., Knowles, J. & Kell, D. B. (2005). Computational cluster validation in post-genomic data analysis. *Bioinformatics*, **21**(15), 3201–3212.

Harbottle, G. (1976). Neutron activation analysis in archaeology. *Radiochemistry*, **3**, 33–72.

Harbottle, G., Sayre, E. V. & Abascal R. (1976). *Neutron Activation Analysis of Thin Orange Pottery*. Upton, NY: Brookhaven National Lab.

Hastie, T., Tibshirani, R., Sherlock, G., Eisen, M., Brown, P. & Botstein, D. (1999). *Imputing Missing Data for Gene Expression Arrays*. Technical report, Stanford University Statistics Department. https://hastie.su.domains/Papers/missing.pdf.

Hawkins, D. M. (1980). *Identification of Outliers*. London: Chapman & Hall.

Heller, K. A. (2007). Efficient Bayesian methods for clustering. PhD thesis, Gatsby Computational Neuroscience Unit, University College London, UK.

Heller, K. A. & Ghahramani, Z. (2005). Bayesian hierarchical clustering. In L. De Raedt and S. Wrobel, eds., *Proceedings of the 22nd International Conference on Machine Learning*. New York: Association for Computing Machinery, pp. 297–304.

Hennig, C. (2015). What are the true clusters? *Pattern Recognition Letters*, **64**, 53–62.

Hennig, C., Meila, M., Murtagh, F. & Rocci, R., eds. (2015). *Handbook of Cluster Analysis*. New York: Chapman & Hall.

Hintze, J. L. & Nelson, R. D. (1998). Violin plots: A box plot-density trace synergism. *American Statistician*, **52**(2), 181–184.

Honaker, J., King, G. & Blackwell, M. (2011). Amelia II: A program for missing data. *Journal of Statistical Software*, **45**(7), 1–47.

Hubert, L. & Arabie, P. (1985). Comparing partitions. *Journal of Classification*, **2**(1), 193–218.

Hubert, M. & Vanden Branden, K. (2003). Robust methods for partial least squares regression. *Journal of Chemometrics*, **17**(10), 537–549.

Hubert, M. & Engelen, S. (2004). Robust PCA and classification in biosciences. *Bioinformatics*, **20**(11), 1728–1736.

Hubert, M., Rousseeuw, P. J. & Vanden Branden, K. (2005). ROBPCA: A new approach to robust principal component analysis. *Technometrics*, **47**(1), 64–79.

Hunt, A. M. W. & Speakman, R. J. (2015). Portable XRF analysis of archaeological sediments and ceramics. *Journal of Archaeological Science*, **53**, 626–638.

Islam, M. H., Kondo, N., Ogawa, Y., Fujiura, T., Suzuki, T. & Fujitani, S. (2018). Interval partial least squares (iPLS) regression approach to predict hatching time of chick. *International Journal of Experimental Spectroscopic Techniques*, **3**(1), article 014. https://doi.org/10.35840/2631-505X/8514.

Jain, A. K. & Dubes, R. C. (1988). *Algorithms for Clustering Data, Vol. 3*. Englewood Cliffs, NJ: Prentice Hall College Division.

Jajuga, K. & Walesiak, M. (2000). Standardization of data set under different measurement scales. In R. Decker and W. Gaul, eds., *Classification and Information Processing at the Turn of the Millennium: Studies in Classification, Data Analysis, and Knowledge Organization*. Berlin: Springer, pp. 105–112.

Joyce, A., Elam, J., Glascock, M. D., Neff, H. & Winter, M. (1995). Exchange implications of obsidian source analysis from the lower Rio Verde Valley, Oaxaca, Mexico. *Latin American Antiquity*, **6**(1), 3–15.

Kampstra, P. (2008). Beanplot: A boxplot alternative for visual comparison of distributions. *Journal of Statistical Software, Code Snippets*, **28**(1), 1–9.

Kass, R. E. & Raftery, A. E. (1995). Bayes factors. *Journal of the American Statistical Association*, **90**(430), 773–795.

Kaufman, L. & Rousseeuw, P. J. (2005). *Finding Groups in Data: An Introduction to Cluster Analysis*. Hoboken, NJ: Wiley-Interscience.

Konstorum, A., Jekel, N., Vidal, E. & Laubenbacher, R. (2018). Comparative analysis of linear and nonlinear dimension reduction techniques on mass cytometry data. *bioRxiv*, 1–15.

Kropko, J., Goodrich, B., Gelman, A. & Hill, J. (2014). Multiple imputation for continuous and categorical data: Comparing joint multivariate normal and conditional approaches. *Political Analysis*, **22**(4), 497–519.

Kucheryavskiy, S. (2020). mdatools – R package for chemometrics. *Chemometrics and Intelligent Laboratory Systems*, **198**, 103937.

Lazzari, M., Pereyra Domingorena, L., Stoner, W. D., Scattolin, M. C., Korstanje, M. A. & Glascock, M. D. (2017). Compositional data supports decentralized model of artefact production and circulation in the pre-Columbian Andes. *Proceedings of the National Academy of Sciences*, **114**(20), E3917–E3926.

Leardi, R. (2000). Application of genetic algorithm-PLS for feature selection in spectral data sets. *Journal of Chemometrics*, **14**(5–6), 643–655.

Lebret, R., Lovleff, S., Langrognet, F., Biernacki, C., Celeux, G. & Govaert, G. (2015). Rmixmod: The R package of the model-based unsupervised, supervised, and semi-supervised classification Mixmod library. *Journal of Statistical Software*, **67**(6), 1–29.

Liland, K. H. & Indahl, U. G. (2020). *Package "EMSC": Extended Multiplicative Signal Correction*. https://cran.r-project.org/web/packages/EMSC/EMSC.pdf (accessed August 22, 2020).

Litton, C. D. & Buck, C. E. (1995). The Bayesian approach to the interpretation of archaeological data. *Archaeometry*, **37**(1), 1–24.

López-García, P., Argote, D. L. & Beirnaert, C. (2019). Chemometric analysis of Mesoamerican obsidian sources. *Quaternary International*, **510**, 100–118.

López-García, P., Argote-Espino, D. & Facevicova K. (2018). Statistical processing of compositional data: The case of ceramic samples from the archaeological site of Xalasco, Tlaxcala, Mexico. *Journal of Archaeological Sciences: Reports*, **19**, 100–114.

López-García, P. A., Argote, D. L. & Thrun, M. C. (2020). Projection-based classification of chemical groups for provenance analysis of archaeological materials. *IEEE Access*, **8**, 152439–152451.

López-García, P. A., García-Gómez, V. H., Acosta-Ochoa, G. & Argote, D. L. (2024). Semi-supervised classification to determine the provenance of archaeological obsidian samples. *Archaeometry*, **66**(1), 142–159.

Lötsch, J., Lerch, F., Djaldetti, R., Tegder, I. & Ultsch, A. (2018). Identification of disease-distinct complex biomarker patterns by means of unsupervised machine-learning using an interactive R toolbox (Umatrix). *Big Data Analytics*, **3**(1), article 5. https://doi.org/10.1186/s41044-018-0032-1.

Lu, B., Morgan, S. P., Crowe, J. A. & Stockford, I. M. (2006). Comparison of methods for reducing the effects of scattering in spectrophotometry. *Applied Spectroscopy*, **60**(10), 1157–1166.

Martens, H. & Stark, E. (1991). Extended multiplicative signal correction and spectral interference subtraction: New preprocessing methods for near infrared spectroscopy. *Journal of Pharmaceutical and Biomedical Analysis*, **9**(8), 625–635.

Martens, H., Nielsen, J. P. & Søren, B. E. (2003). Light scattering and light absorbance separated by extended multiplicative signal correction: Application to near-infrared transmission analysis of powder mixtures. *Analytical Chemistry*, **75**(3), 394–404.

Martín-Fernández, J. A., Barceló-Vidal, C. & Pawlowsky-Glahn, V. (2000). Zero replacement in compositional data sets. In H. A. L. Kiers, J. P. Rasson, P. J. F. Groenen and M. Shader, eds., *Data Analysis, Classification, and Related Methods: Studies in Classification, Data Analysis, and Knowledge Organization*. Berlin: Springer, pp. 155–160.

Martín-Fernández, J. A., Buxeda i Garrigós, J. & Pawlowsky-Glahn, V. (2015). Logratio analysis in archaeometry: Principles and methods. In J. A. Barcelo and I. Bogdanovic, eds., *Mathematics and Archaeology*. Boca Raton, FL: CRC Press, pp. 178–189.

Mateu-i-Figueras, G. & Daunis-i-Estadella, J. (2008). Compositional amalgamations and balances: A critical approach. https://dugi-doc.udg.edu/handle/10256/738.

Maugis, C., Celeux G. & Martin-Magniette M. L. (2009). Variable selection for clustering with Gaussian mixture models. *Biometrics*, **65**(3), 701–709.

McLachlan, G. & Peel, D. (2000). *Finite Mixture Models*. New York: John Wiley & Sons.

Millhauser, J. K., Fargher, L. F., Heredia Espinoza, V. Y. & Blanton, R. E. (2015). The geopolitics of obsidian supply in postclassic Tlaxcallan: A portable X-ray fluorescence study. *Journal of Archaeological Science*, **58**, 133–146.

Millhauser, J. K., Rodríguez-Alegría, E. & Glascock, M. D. (2011). Testing the accuracy of portable X-ray fluorescence to study Aztec and Colonial obsidian supply at Xaltocan, Mexico. *Journal of Archaeological Science*, **38**(11), 3141–3152.

Milligan, G. W. & Cooper, M. C. (1988). A study of standardization of variables in cluster analysis. *Journal of Classification*, **5**, 181–204.

Mitchell, T. J. & Beauchamp, J. J. (1988). Bayesian variable selection in linear regression. *Journal of the American Statistical Association*, **83**(404), 1023–1032.

Moholy-Nagy, H., Meierhoff, J., Golitko, M. & Kestle, C. (2013). An analysis of pXRF obsidian source attributions from Tikal, Guatemala. *Latin American Antiquity*, **24**(1), 72–97.

Mörchen, F. (2006). Time series knowledge mining. Marburg, Germany: Görich and Weiershäuser.

Munita, C. S., Toyota, R. G., Oliveira, P. M. S., Neves, E. G., Demartini, C. C. & Schaan, D. P. (2011). Chapter 7 Chemical characterization of Marajoara pottery. In International Atomic Energy Agency, ed., *Nuclear Techniques for Cultural Heritage Research*. IAEA Radiation Technology Series No. 2. Vienna: International Atomic Energy Agency (IAEA), pp. 133–146.

Muñoz, J. & Amón, I. (2013). Técnicas para detección de outliers multivariantes. *Revista en Telecomunicaciones e Informática*, **3**(5), 11–25.

Murphy, K. & Murphy, T. B. (2020). Gaussian parsimonious clustering models with covariates and a noise component. *Advances in Data Analysis and Classification*, **14**, 293–325.

Murphy, T. B., Dean, N. & Raftery, A. E. (2010). Variable selection and updating in model-based discriminant analysis for high-dimensional data with food authenticity applications. *Annals of Applied Statistics*, **4**(1), 396–421.

Murtagh, F. (2004). On ultrametricity, data coding, and computation. *Journal of Classification*, **21**(2), 167–184.

Nash, J. F. (1951). Non-cooperative games. *Annals of Mathematics*, **54**, 286–295.

Nørgaard, L., Saudland, A., Wagner, J., Nielsen, J. P., Munck, L. & Engelsen, S. B. (2000). Interval partial least squares regression (iPLS): A comparative chemometric study with an example from near-infrared spectroscopy. *Applied Spectroscopy*, **54**(3), 413–419.

Nurunnabi, A., Belton, D. & West, G. (2012). Diagnostic-robust statistical analysis for local surface fitting in 3D point cloud data. *ISPRS Annals of the Photogrammetry, Remote Sensing and Spatial Information Sciences*, **1–3**, 269–274.

Palarea-Albaladejo, J. & Martín-Fernández, J. A. (2015). zCompositions – R package for multivariate imputation of left-censored data under a compositional approach. *Chemometrics and Intelligent Laboratory Systems*, **143**, 85–96.

Palarea-Albaladejo, J., Martín-Fernández, J. A. & Gómez-García, J. (2007). A parametric approach for dealing with compositional rounded zeros. *Mathematical Geology*, **39**(7), 625–645.

Papageorgiou, I. & Liritzis, I. (2007). Multivariate mixture of normals with unknown number of components: An application to cluster neolithic ceramics from Aegean and Asia Minor using portable XRF. *Archaeometry*, **49**(4), 795–813.

Papageorgiou, I., Baxter, M. J. & Cau, M. A. (2001). Model-based cluster analysis of artefact compositional data. *Archaeometry*, **43**(4), 571–588.

Partovi Nia, V. (2009). Fast high-dimensional Bayesian classification and clustering. PhD thesis, Ecole Polytechnique Federale de Lasuanne, Switzerland.

Partovi Nia, V. & Davison, A. C. (2012). High-dimensional Bayesian clustering with variable selection: The R package bclust. *Journal of Statistical Software*, **47**(5), 1–22.

Partovi Nia, V. & Davison, A. C. (2015). *Package "bclust": Bayesian Hierarchical Clustering Using Spike and Slab Models*. https://cran.microsoft .com/snapshot/2017-07-05/web/packages/bclust/bclust.pdf (accessed January 15, 2020).

Pawlowsky-Glahn, V. & Egozcue, J. J. (2011). Exploring compositional data with the CoDa-dendrogram. *Austrian Journal of Statistics*, **40**(1–2), 103–113.

Pawlowsky-Glahn, V. & Egozcue, J. J. (2006). Compositional data and their analysis: An introduction. In A. Buccianti, G. Mateu-Figueras, and V. Pawlowsky-Glahn, eds., *Compositional Data Analysis in the Geosciences: From Theory to Practice*. Special Publication Vol. 264. London: Geological Society, pp. 1–10.

Pawlowsky-Glahn, V., Egozcue, J. J. & Tolosana-Delgado, R. (2015). *Modelling and Analysis of Compositional Data*. Chichester, UK: Wiley.

Pielou, E. C. (1984). *The Interpretation of Ecological Data: A Primer on Classification and Ordination*. New York: Wiley-Interscience.

Raftery, A. E. & Dean, N. (2006). Variable selection for model-based clustering. *Journal of the American Statistical Association*, **101**(473), 168–178.

Rand, W. M. (1971). Objective criteria for the evaluation of clustering methods. *Journal of the American Statistical Association*, **66**(336), 846–850.

R Development Core Team. (2011). *R: A Language and Environment for Statistical Computing*. Vienna: R Foundation for Statistical Computing. www.R-project.org (accessed November 24, 2016).

Reimann, C., Filzmoser, P. & Garrett, R. G. (2002). Factor analysis applied to regional geochemical data: Problems and possibilities. *Applied Geochemistry*, **17**(3), 185–206.

Reyment, R. A. & Savazzi, S. (1999). *Aspects of Multivariate Statistical Analysis in Geology*. Amsterdam: Elsevier.

Rousseau, R. M. (2001). Concept of the influence coefficient. *Rigaku Journal*, **18**(1), 8–21.

Rousseeuw, P. J. (1987). Silhouettes: A graphical aid to the interpretation and validation of cluster analysis. *Journal of Computational and Applied Mathematics*, **20**, 53–65.

Rousseeuw, P. J. & Hubert, M. (2017). Anomaly detection by robust statistics. *WIREs Data Mining and Knowledge Discovery*, **8**(2), e1236. https://doi.org/10.1002/widm.1236.

Rousseeuw, P. J. & van Driessen, K. (1999). A fast algorithm for the minimum covariance determinant estimator. *Technometrics*, **41**(3), 212–223.

Rousseeuw, P. J. & van Zomeren, B. C. (1990). Unmasking multivariate outliers and leverage points. *Journal of the American Statistical Association*, **85**(411), 633–639.

Salem, N. & Hussein, S. (2019). Data dimensional reduction and principal components analysis. *Procedia Computer Science*, **163**, 292–299.

Santos, J. O., Munita, C. S., Valério, M. E. G., Vergne, C. & Oliveira, P. M. S. (2006). Determination of trace elements in archaeological ceramics and application of kernel density estimates: Implications for the definition of production locations. *Journal of Radioanalytical and Nuclear Chemistry*, **269**(2), 441–445.

Savitzky, A. & Golay, M. J. E. (1964). Smoothing and differentiation of data by simplified least squares procedures. *Analytical Chemistry*, **36**(8), 1627–1639.

Sayre, E. V. (1976). Brookhaven procedures for statistical analysis of multivariate archaeometric data. In *Conference on Applications of Physical Sciences to Medieval Archaeology*, Berkeley and Los Angeles, CA, USA, March 18, 1975. Upton, NY: Office of Scientific and Technical Information, pp. 1–33.

Schafer, R. W. (2011). What is a Savitzky-Golay filter? *IEEE Signal Processing Magazine*, **28**(4), 111–117.

Shackley, M. S. (1995). Sources of archaeological obsidian in the greater American Southwest: An update and quantitative analysis. *American Antiquity*, **60**(3), 531–551.

Speakman, R. (2012). *Evaluation of Bruker's Tracer Family Factory Obsidian Calibration for Handheld Portable XRF Studies of Obsidian*. www.researchgate.net/publication/

256547427_Evaluation_of_Bruker's_Tracer_Family_Factory_Obsidian_C-alibration_for_Handheld_Portable_XRF_Studies_of_Obsidian.

Speakman, R., Glascock, M. D. & Steponaitis, V. P. (2008). Chapter 5 Geochemistry. In J. M. Herbert and T. E. McReynolds, eds., *Woodland Pottery Sourcing in the Carolina Sandhills*. Chapel Hill: University of North Carolina Press, pp. 56–72.

Stekhoven, D. J. & Buehlmann, P. (2012). MissForest: Nonparametric missing value imputation for mixed-type data. *Bioinformatics*, **28**(1), 112–118.

Stevens, A. & Ramirez-Lopez, L. (2015). *Package "prospectr": Miscellaneous Functions for Processing and Sample Selection of Vis-NIR Diffuse Reflectance Data*. https://cran.rproject.org/web/packages/prospectr/prospectr.pdf (accessed April 24, 2017).

Stevens, A., Ramirez-Lopez, L. & Hans, G. (2022). *Package "prospectr": Miscellaneous Functions for Processing and Sample Selection of Spectroscopic Data Version 0.2.4*. https://mran.microsoft.com/web/packages/prospectr/prospectr.pdf (accessed April 17, 2022).

Tadesse, M. G., Naijun, S. & Vannucci, M. (2005). Bayesian variable selection in clustering high-dimensional data. *Journal of the American Statistical Association*, **100**(470), 602–617.

Tanasi, D., Tykot, R. H., Pirone, F. & McKendry, E. (2017). Provenance study of prehistoric ceramics from Sicily: A comparative study between pXRF and XRF. *Open Archaeology*, **3**, 222–234.

Templ, M., Alfons, A. & Filzmoser, P. (2012). Exploring incomplete data using visualization techniques. *Advances in Data Analysis and Classification*, **6**, 29–47.

Thrun, M. C. (2018). *Projection-Based Clustering through Self-Organization and Swarm Intelligence: Combining Cluster Analysis with the Visualization of High-Dimensional Data*. Wiesbaden: Springer Vieweg.

Thrun, M. C. (2020). Improving the sensitivity of statistical testing for cluster-ability with mirrored-density plot. In D. Archambault, I. Nabney, and J. Peltonen, eds., *Machine Learning Methods in Visualisation for Big Data*. Norrköping, Sweden: Eurographics Association.

Thrun, M. C. (2021a). Distance-based clustering challenges for unbiased benchmarking studies. *Scientific Reports*, **11**, 18988.

Thrun, M. C. (2021b). The exploitation of distance distributions for clustering. *International Journal of Computational Intelligence and Applications*, **20**(3), 2150016.

Thrun, M. C. (2022). Identification of explainable structures in data with a human-in-the-loop. *German Journal of Artificial Intelligence (Künstl Intelligenz)*, **36**, 297–301.

Thrun, M. C. & Stier, Q. (2021). Fundamental clustering algorithms suite. *SoftwareX*, **13**, 100642.

Thrun, M. C. & Ultsch, A. (2020a). Uncovering high-dimensional structures of projections from dimensionality reduction methods. *MethodsX*, **7**, 101093.

Thrun, M. C. & Ultsch, A. (2020b). Clustering benchmark datasets exploiting the fundamental clustering problems. *Data in Brief*, **30**(C), 105501.

Thrun, M. C. & Ultsch, A. (2021a). Swarm intelligence for self-organized clustering. *Artificial Intelligence*, **290**, 103237.

Thrun, M. C. & Ultsch, A. (2021b). Using projection-based clustering to find distance- and density-based clusters in high-dimensional data. *Journal of Classification*, **38**, 280–312.

Thrun, M. C., Gehlert, T. & Ultsch, A. (2020a). Analyzing the fine structure of distributions. *PLoS One*, **15**(10), e0238835.

Thrun, M. C., Lerch, F., Lötsch, J. & Ultsch, A. (2016). Visualization and 3D printing of multivariate data of biomarkers. In V. Skala, ed., *24th International Conference in Central Europe on Computer Graphics, Visualization and Computer Vision (WSCG)*. Plzen, Czech Republic: Computer Science Research Notes (CSRN)/University of West Bohemia, pp. 7–16.

Thrun, M. C., Märte, J. & Stier, Q. (2023). Analyzing quality measurements for dimensionality reduction. *Machine Learning and Knowledge Extraction*, **5**(3), 1076–1118.

Thrun, M. C., Pape, F. & Ultsch, A. (2020b). Interactive machine learning tool for clustering in visual analytics. In *7th IEEE International Conference on Data Science and Advanced Analytics (DSAA 2020)*. Sydney, Australia: IEEE, pp. 672–680.

Thrun, M. C., Pape, F. & Ultsch, A. (2021). Conventional displays of structures in data compared with interactive projection-based clustering (IPBC). *International Journal of Data Science and Analytics*, **12**(3), 249–271.

Todorov, V. (2020). *Package "rrcov": Scalable Robust Estimators with High Breakdown Point*. https://cran.r-project.org/web/packages/rrcov/rrcov.pdf (accessed September 24, 2020).

Todorov, V. & Filzmoser, P. (2009). An object-oriented framework for robust multivariate analysis. *Journal of Statistical Software*, **32**(3), 1–47.

Todorov, V., Templ, M. & Filzmoser, P. (2011). Detection of multivariate outliers in business survey data with incomplete information. *Advances in Data Analysis and Classification*, **5**(1), 37–56.

Tubb, A., Parker, A. J. & Nickless, G. (1980). The analysis of Romano-British pottery by atomic absorption spectrophotometry. *Archaeometry*, **22**(2), 153–171.

Tukey, J. W. (1977). *Exploratory Data Analysis*. Reading, MA: Addison-Wesley.

Ultsch, A. (1995). Self-organizing neural networks perform different from statistical k-means clustering. In *Proceedings of the Society for Information and Classification (GFKL)*, Vol. 1995. Basel, Switzerland, March 8–10. www.researchgate.net/publication/228827060_Self_organizing_neural_networks_perform_different_from_statistical_k-means_clustering.

Ultsch, A. (1999). Data mining and knowledge discovery with emergent self-organizing feature maps for multivariate time series. In E. Oja and S. Kaski, eds., *Kohonen Maps*. Amsterdam: Elsevier Science B.V., pp. 33–46.

Ultsch, A. (2000). Clustering with dataBots. In *Proceedings of the International Conference in Advances in Intelligent Systems Theory and Applications (AISTA)*. Canberra, Australia: IEEE ACT Section, pp. 99–104.

Ultsch, A. (2003). *U*-matrix: A Tool to Visualize Clusters in High Dimensional Data*. Technical report 36. Department of Mathematics and Computer Science, University of Marburg, Germany. www.cs.ubbcluj.ro/~gabis/DocDiplome/SOM/ultsch03ustar.pdf (accessed April 14, 2024).

Ultsch, A. (2005). Pareto density estimation: A density estimation for knowledge discovery. In D. Baier and K. D. Werrnecke, eds., *Innovations in Classification, Data Science, and Information Systems*, Vol. 27. Berlin: Springer, pp. 91–100.

Ultsch, A. & Lötsch, J. (2017). Machine-learned cluster identification in high-dimensional data. *Journal of Biomedical Informatics*, **66**(C), 95–104.

Ultsch, A. & Siemon, H. P. (1990). Kohonen's self-organizing feature maps for exploratory data analysis. In *Proceedings of the International Neural Network Conference*. Paris, France: Kluwer Academic Press, pp. 305–308.

Ultsch, A. & Thrun, M. C. (2017). Credible visualizations for planar projections. In *12th International Workshop on Self-Organizing Maps and Learning Vector Quantization, Clustering and Data Visualization (WSOM 2017)*, Vol. 1. Nancy, France: IEEE, pp. 256–260.

Ultsch, A., Thrun, M. C., Hansen-Goos, O. & Lötsch, J. (2015). Identification of molecular fingerprints in human heat pain thresholds by use of an interactive mixture model R toolbox (AdaptGauss). *International Journal of Molecular Sciences*, **16**(10), 25897–25911.

van Buuren, S. & Groothuis-Oudshoorn, C. (2011). MICE: Multivariate imputation by chained equations in R. *Journal of Statistical Software*, **45**(3), 1–67.

Van den Boogaart, K. G. & Tolosana-Delgado, R. (2013). *Analyzing Compositional Data with R*. Berlin: Springer-Verlag.

Van der Maaten, L. & Hinton, G. (2008). Visualizing data using t-SNE. *Journal of Machine Learning Research*, **9**(86), 2579–2605.

Van der Maaten, L. J., Postma, E. O. & van den Herik, H. J. (2009). *Dimensionality Reduction: A Comparative Review*. Technical report 2009–005. Tilburg Centre for Creative Computing, Tilburg University, The Netherlands.

Van Loco, J., Elskens, M., Croux, C. & Beernaert, H. (2002). Linearity of calibration curves: Use and misuse of the correlation coefficient. *Accreditation and Quality Assurance*, **7**, 281–285.

Varmuza, K. & Filzmoser, P. (2009). *Introduction to Multivariate Statistical Analysis in Chemometrics*. Boca Raton, FL: CRC Press.

Venna, J., Peltonen, J., Nybo, K., Aidos, H. & Kaski, S. (2010). Information retrieval perspective to nonlinear dimensionality reduction for data visualization. *Journal of Machine Learning Research*, **11**, 451–490.

Verboven, S. & Hubert, M. (2005). LIBRA: A MATLAB library for robust analysis. *Chemometrics and Intelligent Laboratory Systems*, **75** (2), 127–136.

Verleysen, M., Francois, D., Simon, G. & Wertz, V. (2003). On the effects of dimensionality on data analysis with neural networks. In J. Mira and J. R. Álvarez, eds., *International Work-Conference on Artificial Neural Networks IWANN 2003: Artificial Neural Nets Problem Solving Methods*. Berlin: Springer, pp. 105–112.

Vu, T. N., Valkenborg, D., Smets, K., Verwaest, K. A., Dommisse, R., Lemière, F., Verschoren, A., Goethals, B. & Laukens, K. (2011). An integrated workflow for robust alignment and simplified quantitative analysis of NMR spectrometry data. *BMC Bioinformatics*, **12**, 405.

Wang, L. L., Lin, Y. W., Wang, X. F., Xiao, N., Xu, Y. D., Li, H. D. & Xu, Q. S. (2018). A selective review and comparison for interval variable selection in spectroscopic modelling. *Chemometrics and Intelligent Laboratory Systems*, **172**, 229–240.

Wang, S. & Zhu, J. (2008). Variable selection for model-based high-dimensional clustering and its application to microarray data. *Biometrics*, **64**(2), 440–448.

Wehrens, R. (2011). *Chemometrics with R: Multivariate Data Analysis in the Natural Science and Life Sciences*. Berlin: Springer-Verlag.

Weigand, P. C., Harbottle, G. & Sayre, E. V. (1977). Chapter 2 Turquoise sources and source analysis: Mesoamerica and the Southwestern U.S.A. In T. K. Earle and J. E. Ericson, eds., *Exchange Systems in Prehistory*. New York: Academic Press, pp. 15–34.

Wilke, C. O. (2019). *Fundamentals of Data Visualization: A Primer on Making Informative and Compelling Figures*. Sebastopol, CA: O'Reilly Media.

Wilkinson, L. & Friendly, M. (2009). The history of the cluster heat map. *American Statistician*, **63**(2), 179–184.

Xie, B., Pan, W. & Shen, X. (2008). Penalized model-based clustering with cluster-specific diagonal covariance matrices and grouped variables. *Electronic Journal of Statistics*, **2**, 168–212.

Cambridge Elements ☰

Current Archaeological Tools and Techniques

Hans Barnard

Cotsen Institute of Archaeology

Hans Barnard was associate adjunct professor in the Department of Near Eastern Languages and Cultures as well as associate researcher at the Cotsen Institute of Archaeology, both at the University of California, Los Angeles. He currently works at the Roman site of Industria in northern Italy and previously participated in archaeological projects in Armenia, Chile, Egypt, Ethiopia, Italy, Iceland, Panama, Peru, Sudan, Syria, Tunisia, and Yemen. This is reflected in the seven books and more than 100 articles and chapters to which he contributed.

Willeke Wendrich

Polytechnic University of Turin

Willeke Wendrich is Professor of Cultural Heritage and Digital Humanities at the Politecnico di Torino (Turin, Italy). Until 2023 she was Professor of Egyptian Archaeology and Digital Humanities at the University of California, Los Angeles, and the first holder of the Joan Silsbee Chair in African Cultural Archaeology. Between 2015 and 2023 she was Director of the Cotsen Institute of Archaeology, with which she remains affiliated. She managed archaeological projects in Egypt, Ethiopia, Italy, and Yemen, and is on the board of the International Association of Egyptologists, Museo Egizio (Turin, Italy), the Institute for Field Research, and the online UCLA Encyclopedia of Egyptology.

About the Series

Cambridge University Press and the Cotsen Institute of Archaeology at UCLA collaborate on this series of Elements, which aims to facilitate deployment of specific techniques by archaeologists in the field and in the laboratory. It provides readers with a basic understanding of selected techniques, followed by clear instructions how to implement them, or how to collect samples to be analyzed by a third party, and how to approach interpretation of the results.

COTSEN INSTITUTE OF
ARCHAEOLOGY AT UCLA

Cambridge Elements $^{\equiv}$

Current Archaeological Tools and Techniques

Elements in the Series

Printed in the United States
by Baker & Taylor Publisher Services